THE PRIEST

THE PRIEST

His Inner Life and His Educational, Sacerdotal, and Pastoral Work

Metropolitan Michael Constantinides of Corinth

ATHENS, 1946

Translated into English by
Christopher Tripoulas and Christopher Vrettos

Holy Cross Orthodox Press

Brookline, Massachusetts

With thanks to V. Rev. Anthony Falsarella (1958-2023), of blessed memory, who shepherded the final versions of this text to their completion. May his memory be eternal!

Published by Holy Cross Orthodox Press
Hellenic College, Inc.
50 Goddard Avenue
Brookline, MA 02445

ISBN 978-1-935317-32-6

Library of Congress Cataloging-in-Publication Data

Michael, Archbishop of North and South America, 1892-1958.
[Hiereus. English]
The priest : his inner life and his educational, sacerdotal, and pastoral work / Metropolitan Michael Constantinides of Corinth ; translated into English by Christopher Tripoulas and Christopher Vrettos.
pages cm

ISBN 978-1-935317-32-6
1. Orthodox Eastern Church--Clergy. 2. Orthodox Eastern Church--Doctrines. 3. Pastoral care. I. Tripoulas, Christopher, translator. II. Vrettos, Christopher, translator. III. Title.
BX341.5.M534 2014
262'.1419--dc23
2013042571

Table of Contents

Part 3 – The Priest and Children

Part 4 – The Sanctificational Work of a Priest

Part 5 – The Pastoral Work of a Priest

FOREWORD

My beloved predecessor, Archbishop Michael, was one of the most prominent Christian leaders of the twentieth century. From 1949 to 1958, he served as the Greek Orthodox Archbishop of North and South America. Prior to that, he served as the Metropolitan of Corinth from 1939 to 1949, as Dean of the Cathedral of Saint Sophia in London from 1927 to 1939, and as Chancellor of the Archdiocese of Athens and All Greece from 1923 to 1927.

Throughout his life's ministry, he exhibited many virtues and qualities that endeared him to countless individuals across the globe — the foremost being his sense of deep faith and pastoral sensitivity, as well as his distinct ability to convey complex theological ideas in a loving manner that was practical, relatable, and understandable. This visionary Archbishop had an incredibly calm, peaceful, and humble disposition, and personified what it meant to be a shepherd in the modern age.

Many of our Archdiocesan ministries and institutions were first established by this gifted hierarch of our Church. Archbishop Michael pioneered a new era in the presence and witness of the Greek Orthodox Archdiocese of America. With his message of living an authentic life in Christ, he laid the groundwork for a successful foundation, upon which we continue to build on today as the most dynamic Eparchy of the Ecumenical Throne of Constantinople. In striving to instill a sacred deposit of the Orthodox faith in the heart and conscience of his flock, this pious servant of the Lord has a universality to his archpastoral ministry that is widely respected — as is affirmed by his loving service, both within the United States and abroad.

Through this present volume entitled "The Priest," which has been translated into English for the centennial year of our Sacred Archdiocese, the legacy and spirit of this beloved Archbishop of America continues to inspire us as we move forward in our collective journey as a body of believers in the United States. This publication is ultimately an expression of Archbishop Michael's genuine love, care, and compassion for his flock. These pages make evident that the very core of his daily ministry was always the spiritual wellbeing and transformation of clergy and laity alike.

The reader of this rich publication will be astonished with the extent to which Archbishop Michael's work remains just as relevant in our contemporary society as it did during his time. I personally share his desire to equip our clergy with the wisdom and experience of the Orthodox Church in order that they might have the best tools needed to confront the various challenges of their priestly ministry. The treasure-trove of pastoral riches that is contained in this work addresses today's issues in a manner that is most conducive to the spiritual prosperity of the devout faithful of our Archdiocese. May the memory of this ever-blessed hierarch be eternally honored and remembered by all those who study this handbook and who fully embrace the heartfelt devotion that Archbishop Michael expressed during his lifetime for the Lord and His Church, especially in America.

† ELPIDOPHOROS
Archbishop of America

INTRODUCTION
TO THE ENGLISH TRANSLATION

His Eminence, Michael, the late Archbishop of North and South America is a hierarch and man of God that holds a special place in the hearts of all here at Saint Basil Academy. The academy is the archbishop's final resting place, that he personally chose. He also in his days as archbishop found a place of respite and spiritual reinvigoration here during his tenure as the hierarchical leader of the Church in the western hemisphere.

His Eminence was a man of many extraordinary facets, all of which brought the message of our Lord, Jesus Christ to the faithful and clergy to wherever he served. He led by example and not just words, changing the lives of countless people.

One example of his strength and courage occurred during the Second World War. The German occupiers in 1943 were going to execute the entire male population of Corinth that were over the age of twelve in reprisal for the death of a German soldier by members of the resistance. Archbishop Michael learning about this as he was on a pastoral visit to a nearby village, asked a man with a motorcycle to rush him to the execution site. Arriving as the firing squad was assembling, Archbishop Michael took a position between the squad of soldiers and those condemned. He spoke to the Germans in their native tongue and stated that if they are to carry out the execution, he would be the first to be shot. As he stood there unflinchingly, the German squad lowered their rifles, and a massacre was avoided. He was a constant model to the clergy and faithful during the times of war, both the Second World War and the immediately following of the Greek Civil War, constantly extending love, comfort, guidance, and education.

Archbishop Michael was a man of learning, having not only his secondary education, but attending the Patriarchal Seminary in Halki along with the

Theological Academies in both Kiev and St. Petersburg, Russia. Through his studies, he became prolific in at least five languages that aided him in his challenging and diverse ministry throughout his life. His ordination saw him assume higher responsibilities first as the metropolis preacher in Maronia, Greece. Following this he served as the chancellor of the Archdiocese of Athens from 1923-1927. In 1927, he was appointed as the Dean of Saint Sophia Cathedral in London, England. Throughout his posts he was an ardent student learning from those around him including other confessions, assessing their practices, and finally implementing those ideas and practices that would work within an Orthodox context.

In London, he flourished as a man of God. Not only did he perform his pastoral duties selflessly, but also found time to write prolifically. This present volume was initially based on many of his experiences serving in the United Kingdom. He wrote several other books, some of which are in use today. He was able to also see how those of the Church of England educated their faithful both young and old, and bring some of those ideas into practice, both in his pastoral assignment in London and then to the Metropolis of Corinth and then to the Archdiocese of North and South America.

Archbishop Michael was a proponent of having the church and faithful adapt to the circumstances it found itself in outside of the homelands and working through these challenges. One example of these challenges was finance. It was his inspired idea to come up with the *Dekadollarion*, or the assessment of $10 per family unit from each community to fund the expanding services and ministries of the archdiocese. The archdiocese had expanded beyond the services of a basic office administration, and now was informing the faithful via a regularly published publication the *Orthodox Observer*, a vibrant youth ministry, religious education, regular pastoral parish visitations, etc. These are services we are used to receiving today, but were implemented through the guidance of Archbishop Michael.

During his short tenure (9 ½ years) as archbishop of North and South America, Archbishop Michael successfully campaigned to have the Orthodox faith recognized as a major faith group on both the state and federal levels in the United States. Before that time, our Orthodox servicemen and others in official duties had their religious preference classified either "Catholic" or

"Protestant," since the Orthodox Church was not afforded a recognized status and thus deprived of the services of Orthodox chaplains. The culmination of this recognition came with the second inauguration of President Dwight Eisenhower in January 1957, when Archbishop Michael was invited to and offered the opening invocation.

The archbishop was also a leader among the religious leaders worldwide. Always active in ecumenical affairs, representing the Orthodox Church, its faith, beliefs and practices; he was elected in 1954 one of the five presidents of the World Council of Churches. This honor and distinction have only been honored a few times in the history of this assembly of religious leaders throughout the world.

His crowning achievement though has always been to his ministry in the western hemisphere. From the time of his enthronement until his premature death, Archbishop Michael was focused on giving his all to the clergy and faithful. It was through his insight and blessing that the Greek Orthodox Youth of America (GOYA) was organized and flourished. This started as a handful of groups and by the end of his tenure spread to chapters throughout the United States. He would always take a special interest in the youth, personally guiding and encouraging them. He was able to place the archdiocese on a firm administrative and financial footing. He spent his time when his schedule permitted staying at Saint Basil Academy in Garrison, New York. Here he had a cottage where he would retreat to as time permitted. He interacted with the students of the college during his visits exhorting and encouraging them as he only could. He always had his eye fixed on what the youth could contribute to the future of the church in America. Finally, when his life came to its premature end, Archbishop Michael was buried at Saint Basil Academy a short distance from his beloved cottage retreat.

His love for the clergy showed no bounds. His personal wisdom on the scriptures, patristics and pastoral experiences were always shared at gatherings of the clergy and also with those preparing for the priesthood at Holy Cross Seminary. He led by establishing a format for our Clergy-Laity Congresses that exists even to present day.

With all that he shared with the clergy and also the faithful, he left us with a number of books he published. This present volume, *The Priest* has sound pastoral advice that applies for the most part today as it did when it was first published and circulated. It is being reprinted not only as a tribute to the guidance that he gave to the priests he so loved, but as an inspiration to the ministry of all who served the archdiocese, he so loved and guided.

May his memory be eternal!

Rev. Father Constantine L. Sitaras
Executive Director
Saint Basil Academy
Garrison, New York

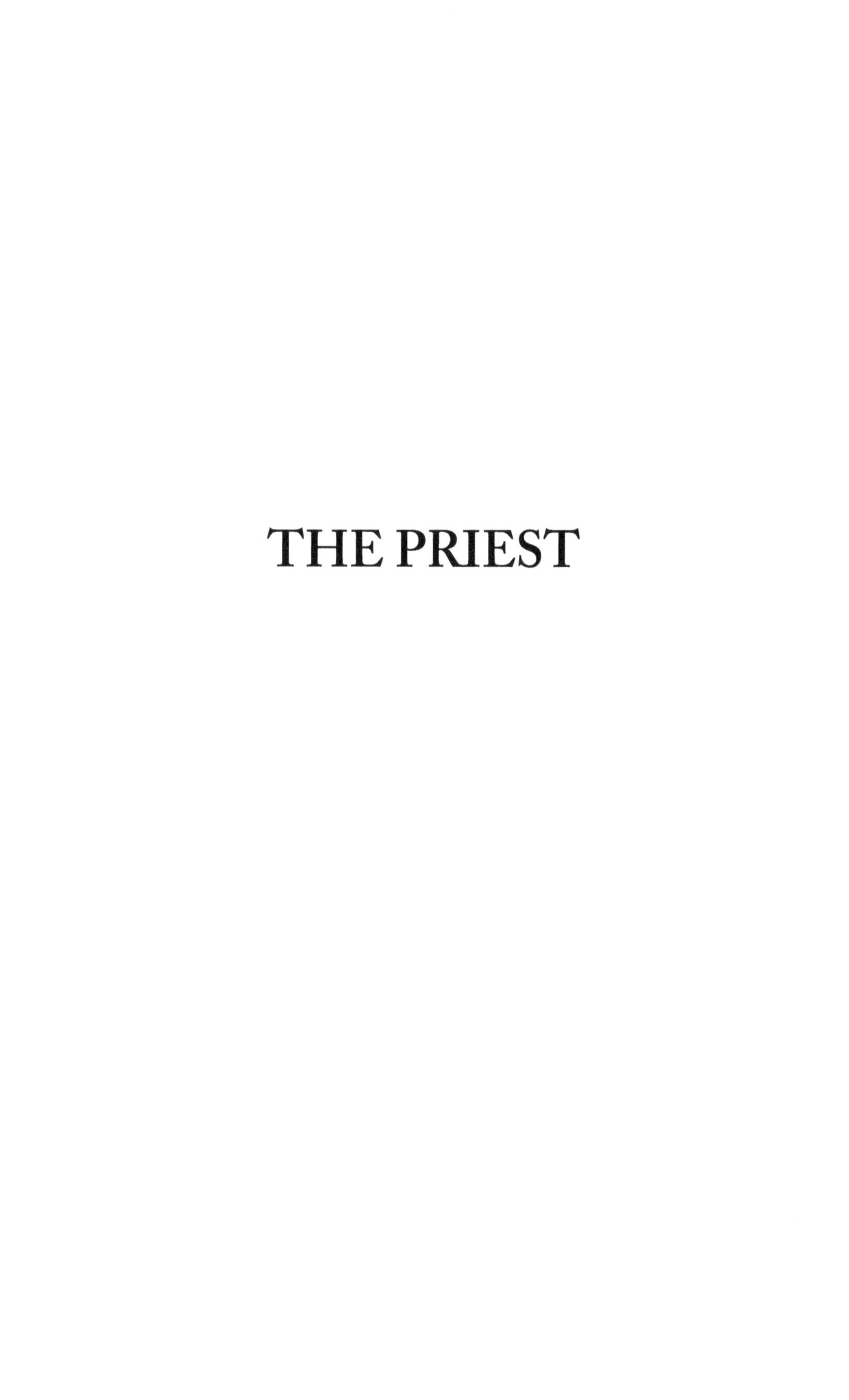

THE PRIEST

FOREWORD
TO THE FIRST EDITION

I wrote this book in my spare time from my parish duties. As the reader will see, this is not a pastoral handbook in the true sense. It is a book that examines what a priest's inner life should be, and it touches upon the most important aspects of his educational, sacerdotal, and pastoral duties. I thought that in its present form, my work—which is devoid of any scholarly claims and completely practical in nature—would attract the interest of my brothers in Christ and prove useful to them in their work of bringing about a rebirth among the faithful, a work that they have already set out upon or will be preparing themselves for in the near future.

In England, where the practical aspect of Christianity is cultivated more than anywhere else, there is a plethora of books dealing with this sort of practical knowledge. Each of the three aspects of priestly service continuously appears individually and collectively in books penned by reputable clergyman who possess an academically solid theological education, lengthy pastoral experience, and deep piety. As a result, a priest has scores of books relating to his work both in and out of the Church. These books, each with their own fair share of circulation, are kept track of and studied by the clergy, who consider it their duty to perfect themselves and continuously seek help in the great task and immense responsibility of assuming the spiritual leadership of the Christian faithful entrusted to them.

Keeping these similar types of works in mind and the terms under which a Greek Orthodox priest is called to work and act—and filled with the deep desire to facilitate to the extent of my meager powers and, if possible, make more efficient the work of my brothers in Christ, who are either already serving the Church or are currently in training in theological schools and seminaries—I proceeded to write this book.

Looking at the efforts being put forth both in Greece and elsewhere in Greek-speaking Orthodox Christian communities worldwide to make Sunday schools a full-fledged institution, I thought it useful to devote a portion of this book to the clergy's catechetical work, and I have attempted to provide instructions that are as informative and useful as possible for successful catechesis, which aims as providing religious instruction to Orthodox Christian youth.

I did not write much on the subject of a priest's sacerdotal work, as this is laid out in the official texts of the Orthodox Church. In the little that I did include regarding this most important of all priestly duties, I concluded by citing practical observations.

I thought it best to dedicate the largest portion of this work to expounding upon the genuinely pastoral work of a clergyman. More than any other aspect, this particular dimension of a priest's *diakonia* ("service") has unfortunately been overlooked by our clergy. This is attributed to a variety of different reasons.

Nonetheless, every objective researcher studying the state of today's Church readily admits that it is at a higher level than it was several decades ago. Sermons are more frequent and systematized, the need to offer the Greek Orthodox youth religious instruction has been recognized, and Sunday schools are being established everywhere. The sacrament of Holy Confession—this unique hospital offering spiritual therapy and rebirth in Christ—has assumed its rightful place. Zealous bishops and priests driven by godly enthusiasm are performing works of exceptional public benefit. Most importantly, all the responsible parties have long since recognized the need to work harder and more continuously to shape a clergy that is in all respects worthy of meeting the challenges of today's world and the issues facing us. If there are any others that are lagging behind in this effort, the movement taking place around them and gaining more and more momentum by the day will push them forward as well, whether they like it or not, to join in the common struggle and fight the good fight.

As I happily follow this auspicious movement, which has recently come to characterize our Church polity, as a trifling and humble worker and servant of the Church I contribute this present work, which may be worth little in value but is rich in good intentions, with the hope that it will be cast as a pebble into the joints and junctions of the building blocks that others more capable and—truth be told—more worthy than I are offering to the great edificational work that constitutes our ecclesiastical rebirth.

FOREWORD

TO THE SECOND EDITION

By the grace of God, we are now proceeding with the second edition of our book *The Priest*, which was first published in Alexandria approximately fourteen years ago, through the sponsorship of the ever-memorable patron of the letters, the great Pope and Patriarch Meletios.

From the very moment that the first edition began to circulate, we saw its many flaws. Even as I was writing it in London amidst the serene and unforgettable atmosphere of the rectory of St. Sophia, I was well aware of the fact that I was not attempting to prepare a work of systematic pastoral training, nor was I planning on offering a work of scholarly merit to our fellow priests in Christ and those planning on joining the clergy in the future. As a result, such a work could not help but be characterized by many flaws.

The purpose of this second edition is to offer a practical handbook that is certainly more complete. The improvements made to this current edition include the enrichment of the chapter on passages from the Church fathers—especially the immortal words of St. John Chrysostom in *On the Priesthood*—through the improvement of numerous headings, by revising some of them and adding new ones.

I decided to proceed in printing this second edition for the same reasons that I mentioned in the foreword to the first edition: because texts like this, which deal with a parish priest's work from a practical standpoint and aid him in performing his mission in society (which is so great and of such immense responsibility) are, unfortunately, very rare among us. Whereas priests in Western European countries, especially Great Britain, have at their disposal a plethora of books in which the service of a priest is laid out and studied in a practical manner—in fact, due to the large number of such books, a number so large that it is seemingly unbelievable for us, the priest or candidate for the priesthood considers it his duty to consult with experts about which of these books he ought to choose to help guide him in his service to his fellow Christians, so as to avoid wasting valuable time—unfortunately, such related books rarely ever become available to the public in our Church. One cannot argue that this is due to the lack of interest on behalf of our priests or those interested in becoming men of the cloth. Resounding proof of the fact that there is great interest in reading such practical handbooks lies in the fact that the first edition of this work was purchased so quickly, that the requests of many priests from regions all throughout Greece who contacted me—especially since I assumed episcopal duties in Corinth—were unable to be met due to the fact that the first edition had long since gone out of circulation.

If the publication of handbooks such as this stands as a source of great benefit for our priests, these will be of far greater benefit during the present time period in world events, and especially in light of our long-suffering country's plight. The great war, which we all witnessed with terror and deep anxiety, proved beyond a doubt that in general all the achievements made in science and the arts have made mankind unhappy instead of happy.

Every Christian who has been reborn was absolutely certain that things would end up like this for mankind, which boasted and bragged of its accomplishments and successes in the field of science and had shortsightedly thought it had found the road that would lead us to an earthly paradise of comfort, happiness, and peace.

Now it sees the huge carnage that its deliberate shortsightedness has cost it. Unfortunately, this is not the first time that mankind has seen its hopes utterly destroyed. It has built castles in the sand, and they have collapsed like a stack of cards. But did the same thing not occur prior to the previous World War, when the world once again saw the tower, it wanted to build as high as the sky turn into rubble and ruins? Since the source of the root of evil was revealed back then, and in spite of this, mankind remained incorrigible and unreformed following that terrible storm and insisted upon its old ways, rebuilding its entire castle in the sand once again, what person with any common sense could deny that we would arrive at the complete destruction that took place during this present all-out war? "The wages of sin are death," according to God's true word. Unfortunately, mankind will learn its lesson following a destruction that has never before been seen in the course of human events. What is the lesson that it needs to learn? God Himself came down to earth to teach it to mankind, and to impress upon us that "the Word became flesh." He told us "the kingdom of God is within you." We all bear inside of us the prerequisites for heaven or hell. We are free if we so choose, and we have all the means available to cultivate our inner person and transform him into a true paradise, both for ourselves and for our environment. On the other hand, we are also free to create inside ourselves an inferno of never-ending egotism, hate, and evil. If we leave our heart uncultivated, if we overlook its claims and demands, if we turn all our attention to our intellect, enriching and glorifying it, a hell of passions will automatically arise. When our neglected and overlooked heart overflows with the lava of the passions, at some point this lava will disrupt our inner self, shake it to its core, and in its tide of destruction it will spill over to burn us and anyone else around us that it can reach. "The kingdom of God is within you." Comfort, happiness, and peace have our inner self as their source. Let us go ahead and implement the innovations and discoveries that we have at our disposal. Better yet, let us go ahead and implement these one hundred or one thousand times over, so that we reach a point in our civilization where each one of us has in his possession an unimaginable quantity of gold and silver. Despite all this, if we leave our heart uncultivated, if we do not open its doors so that Jesus Christ, who is "the same yesterday, and today, and forever" may enter, after several years the horrific tragedy of another world war will surely be repeated.

The matter is so simple, yet so complex. The hell that exists inside of us must be turned into heaven. This is the infallible formula that was left to us by Jesus Christ—the only infallible one—who once walked upon the earth for the benefit of mankind. We, the holy clergy, who are His main collaborators, have a sacred mission and imperative duty to bring about this change in ourselves first, and then in others.

The Greek Civil War, which has marred our memories and left a dark shadow on the history of our country, proved beyond the shadow of a doubt that the Greek soul is seriously ill and in grave danger. The atrocities and brutalities committed during that most savage period of infighting call out to us that the soul of our people has not been converted to Christianity, and that their hearts have not been tamed. All that was considered to be associated with people who are by nature barbarous and uncivilized was witnessed to have been committed by our people, despite the fact that we refer to ourselves as "the chosen people," during moments of national delirium.

Now, these ailing people—exhausted from the fever of their recent major battles and crushed by the national and individual challenges facing them, these people who only recently managed to drag themselves out of hunger, nakedness, and disappointment, who are ever suspicious of one another and filled with hatred for each other due to the unforgivable, destructive internal strife taking place among us—must recover, regain their spiritual bearings, and once again become a society living in harmony and mutual understanding and acceptance. How will this be accomplished? How will the hell of hatred and enmity toward our brothers that lies within us be transformed into heaven? Through some sort of social system? Through some specific form of government? Our illness is internal, however. No system or form of government—even the best one—is in a position to cure an ailment of the soul, an internal disease. A good police force is only able to deter crimes and misdemeanors from occurring. However, it is never in a position to institute inner changes in people or ensure that they feel disgust and hate for crimes and trespasses. Only one power has proven itself capable of bringing about man's inner change: divine grace, which draws upon an endless wellspring, which is none other than the perpetual victim sacrificed at Golgotha for the life and salvation of all who believe in Him. Greek Orthodox Christian clergymen are now being called upon to bring about an inner change in the hearts and souls of the Greek Orthodox people. The holy clergy is and remains the only hope for the salvation and prosperity of Greece.

This is why, in the midst of this critical period we are passing through following a civil war that has plunged an entire nation into unspeakable mourning, I decided to proceed with the republication of this work, which deals with the role and work of priests in society. Its purpose is to pique the interest of those who will continue the work of our Savior Jesus Christ, and to make them want to constantly examine their inner self, and to vigilantly watch over it with care, fully roused— "For our struggle is not against flesh and blood, but against the rulers, against the authorities, against the powers of this dark world and against the spiritual forces of evil in the heavenly realms"—that having "put on the whole armor of God," they may create a spiritual life among Christians, without which a Christian is truly said to be "a resounding gong or a clanging cymbal." Moreover, this book aims to inspire them with a fervent zeal to lead the Christian faithful to the brave decision of "stripping yourselves of the old man with his deeds, and putting on the new, him who is renewed unto knowledge, according to the image of Him that created him," and to subsequently watch every step of the faithful, leading them both in the church and in their homes as well.

So, through their words, their example, and the performance of their priestly duties, all of which edify them and lead them onto the path of salvation, the people may realize the ideal on behalf of which we pray extensively, at the instruction of Christ our Shepherd: "Hallowed be Thy name; Thy kingdom come; Thy will be done, on earth as it is in heaven."

In Corinth
February 21, 1945
+ Metropolitan Michael of Corinth

PART 1

THE INNER LIFE OF A PRIEST

CHAPTER 1

The Spirituality of the Priestly Mission

Before we proceed in examining the educational, sacerdotal, and pastoral work of a priest, I consider it worthwhile—in fact, necessary—to say a few words about his inner life and the spiritual condition, so to speak, in which he finds himself and leads his life.

A priest is not like the other mortal men with whom he lives, and whose religious and moral needs he serves. From the moment that the bishop lays his hands upon him and calls upon the Holy Spirit to ordain him to the priesthood, it is understood that he is set aside from the body of the laity, where he previously belonged, and that he severs every tie with his former life and is "set apart for the gospel of God." From that moment on, everything that the Holy Spirit said about Barnabas and Saul holds true for him: "Set apart for me Barnabas and Saul for the work to which I have called them" (Acts 13:2). This is how Christ, the fathers and teachers of the Church understood the role of the priest. "A priest stands in between God and human nature, bringing down divine honors upon us and sending up our supplications," St. John Chrysostom writes. Elsewhere St. John Chrysostom—who surpasses all others in both theory and practice in serving Christ, save for St. Paul the Apostle—notes that "for if anyone will consider how great a thing it is for one, being a man, and compassed with flesh and blood, to be enabled to draw near to that blessed and pure nature, he will then clearly see what great honor the grace of the Spirit has vouchsafed to priests . . . For they who inhabit the earth and make their abode there are entrusted with the administration of things which are in Heaven, and have received an authority which God has not given to angels or archangels" (*On the Priesthood* 3.5, in The Nicene and Post-Nicene Fathers [henceforth NPNF], Series 1, ed. Philip Schaff, 9:46–47; original in Patrologia Graeca [henceforth PG], ed. Jacques-Paul Migne, 48:643).

Inspired by the Holy Spirit, a priest ought to follow in the footsteps of this great teacher and, while dutifully following, learn the methods and means by which to serve mankind. He should not for even a moment forget the basic truth that every external action of which he depends completely and fully on the quality of his inner self.

"Pay attention to yourself," St. Paul writes to Timothy. A priest ought to always have the phrase "pay attention to yourself" on his mind. Only then, when he is vigilantly heeding himself, can he influence others. Only then can he prove himself to be useful and show himself to be the salt of the earth and the light of the world; when he instructs himself first and foremost, places every unruly desire and bad habit under control, and fashions himself into a living example of virtue. We have heard St. John Chrysostom—whose soul was truly as golden as his tongue—speak on the purity that the soul of a priest ought to have: "For the soul of the priest ought to be purer than the very sunbeams, in order that the Holy Spirit may not leave him desolate, in order that he may be able to say, 'Now I live; and yet no longer I, but Christ lives in me'" (NPNF[1] 9:75, modified; PG 48:676). Elsewhere he adds, "The soul of the priest should shine like a light beaming over the whole world" (NPNF[1] 9:76; PG 48:681). Furthermore he states, "Priests are the salt of the earth . . . For the priest ought not only to be thus pure as one who has been dignified with so high a ministry, but very discreet, and skilled in many matters, and to be as well versed in the affairs of this life as they who are engaged in the world, and yet to be free from them all more than the recluses who occupy the mountains" (ibid.). The poverty of the soul cannot be satisfied by noisy external activity that aims at making an impression. On how many occasions have sermons, advanced lessons, charitable work, and in fact pretentious altruism proved unable to turn the souls of men to repentance, renew their hearts, and lead them bound up before the feet of the Divine Savior, despite the initial movement that they ostensibly generate. We often ask ourselves just what exactly is happening here. Seek and you will find, and then you shall be convinced. Those who preach and minister in this way try to save the souls of others, but they overlook their own souls in the midst of all the clamor they cause around the others. A soul that is overlooked and spiritually degenerated, a soul that does not itself first experience spiritual uplifting and does not itself savor the incomparable pleasure of upholding the Lord's commandments above all other pleasures cannot influence the souls of others. It simply creates momentary impressions and sentiments, which do not, however, find their way "even to dividing soul and spirit, joints and marrow" (Heb. 4:12). In other words, this type of ministry resembles a steamboat's noisy paddle, which crashes into the water, creates foam, and disrupts the surfaces of the sea, but whose power cannot reach the bottomless depth of the unparted sea. "Pay attention to yourself"; this is what a priest ought to always keep in mind.

So, it is a priest's duty, as the one who sanctifies the people through the celebration of the holy sacraments, to become "a lamp unto feet and a light to paths," as he was called to do, and to be a spiritual guide for others. It is a priest's imperative duty to always have his sacred calling and mission in sight. St. John Chrysostom writes, "For the priestly office is indeed discharged on earth, but it ranks among heavenly ordinances; and very naturally so: for neither man, nor angel, nor archangel, nor any other created power, but the Paraclete Himself, instituted this vocation, and persuaded men while still abiding in the flesh to represent the ministry of angels. Wherefore the consecrated priest ought to be as pure as if he were standing in the heavens themselves in the midst of those powers" (NPNF[1] 9:46; PG 48:642). Elsewhere he adds, "It behooves one who undertakes this care to have much understanding, and, before understanding, great grace from God, and uprightness of conduct, and purity of life and superhuman virtue" (NPNF[1] 9:49, modified; PG 48:645). When he knelt before the holy altar in order to become a vessel of the All-Holy Spirit, the priest makes the promise to purify his entire self in the Church. This promise, which completely precludes every earthly care, thought, and connection, ought not and cannot be rejected. The Holy Spirit, which descends upon him through prayer and the laying on of hands by the bishop, places upon his soul an irremovable seal. The right to perform priestly duties may be withheld from him for a period of time or permanently, but he cannot but be a priest for all the days of his life, and this is how he will be judged when he appears before the awesome judgment seat of our just God.

In light of this, a priest is called to be the center of all spirituality, passing this on to those around him—in other words, to all those whose spiritual and moral needs he is charged with serving. A spirit of worldliness and materialism—the two evils that have grabbed hold of every social class, spreading the poison and germs of corruption and decay throughout society in its entirety like a terrible, incurable cancer, and having entered, alas, in some instances into the sacred institution of the Church—is a spirit that should have no place in the soul of a priest. On the contrary, he ought to be a sturdy rock upon which the waves of these two ghastly social ills will crash into and dissolve into steamy foam.

CHAPTER 2

The Dangers of the Priestly Ministry

A priest has all the more duty to direct his undivided attention to his inner spiritual life, because the dangers closing in on him from all directions are many in number and variety, and only through his deep and stable spiritual life will he be able to successfully handle each of them. Of course it holds true for every Christian, but especially for a priest, who is preordained to constantly struggle for the spiritual salvation of his Christians, that "our struggle is not against flesh and blood, but against the rulers, against the authorities, against the powers of this dark world and against the spiritual forces of evil in the heavenly realms" (Eph. 6:12). A priest's mission is to snatch Christians from the insatiable and sharp jaws of the evil one, who "prowls around like a roaring lion looking for someone to devour" (1 Pet. 5:8).

First of all, a priest ought to be able to handle the grave danger that springs from the very insides of his old self. Despite the grace we receive during the sacraments of Baptism and Chrismation, and subsequently during the sacrament of Holy Orders, our old self always exists within us, lying in wait and seeking the right opportunity to appear as our inner master and embarrass us in the eyes of our spiritual children, while in a like manner it neutralizes our ability to benefit and aid our Christian flock in their entirety. St. Paul the Apostle, the colossus of Christian preaching who was taken up to the third heaven and given a foretaste of paradise while still living here on earth, recognizes this danger that he is exposed to from his old self and exclaims, "I discipline my body and keep it under control, lest after preaching to others I myself should be disqualified" (1 Cor. 9:27).

This is why a priest, whose ministry aims at combating the old self that exists within all the members of his flock and wiping it out along with its deeds and desires, has an even greater and more compelling reason to constantly fight against the old self that lies within him, until he manages to deaden it completely. The prevalence of the old self in the instance of an everyday Christian does not leave any deep impression upon his or her acquaintances. On the other hand, the appearance of the old self in the life of a priest and the poor example he sets utterly scandalizes the entire community in which he lives and ministers, and acts to usher in countless evils. Whereas the shortcomings and vices of others are known to a limited group of people at best, with whom they interact on a daily basis, on the contrary, the shortcomings of priests—small as they may be—are noticed by everyone and are magnified in the eyes of the people due to the prominent position that members of the clergy hold in society. St. John Chrysostom writes that "it is quite impossible for the defects of priests to be concealed, but even trifling ones speedily become manifest. So, an athlete, as long as he remains at home, and contends with no one, can dissemble his weakness even if it be very great, but when he strips for the contest, he is easily detected . . . For the faults of ordinary men, being committed as it were in the dark, ruin only those who practice them, but the errors of a man in a conspicuous position, and known to many, inflicts a common injury upon all . . . but if they err in the smallest matters these trifles seem great to others" (NPNF[1] 9:52; PG 48:650). Consider, for instance, how many evils the greatest of all vices, vanity—which is so prevalent among clergy of both the higher and lower orders—brings. The privileged place of the clergy in society; the respect that is afforded to them by the faithful due primarily to their collar and calling; the positions they enjoy in committees, organizations, and associations of all sorts; and the prominent place given to them by others due to their vocation and ministry unfortunately often give rise to vanity among members of the clergy who are lacking in spiritual life, and greatly debase the priestly ministry in the eyes of the people, especially those who are well advanced in leading a religious life. St. John Chrysostom, who tried with all his strength to avoid taking on the priestly ministry on account of the colossal dangers that accompany it, is justified in listing vanity atop this list of dangers: "And first of all is that most terrible rock of vainglory, more dangerous than that of the Sirens, of which the fable-mongers tell such marvelous tales: for many were able to sail past that and escape unscathed; but this is to me so dangerous that even now, when no necessity of any kind impels me into that abyss, I am unable to keep clear of the snare" (NPNF[1] 9:49; PG 48:646).

Then, consider how deeply disgraced the equally great shortcoming of anger can leave a priest. This holy father of the Church has this to say regarding this issue: "For nothing clouds the purity of the reason, and the perspicuity of the mental vision so much as undisciplined wrath, rushing along with violent impetuosity. 'For wrath,' says one, 'destroys even the prudent' [Prov 15:1, LXX]" (NPNF[1] 9:51; PG 48:649).

How many times has this great and terrible beast left the conscience of the faithful in utter dismay, and destroyed entire careers of capable and otherwise successful priests with active ministries? Does it not infect the sanctity of the Divine Liturgy itself when even bishops are unable to control their tempers, oftentimes for miniscule and insignificant reasons? What can be said of avarice, greed, and ravenousness, vices that are in direct conflict with the priestly ministry, whose catchphrase ought to be self-sacrifice and self-denial. For Christ, "being in very nature God, did not consider equality with God something to be grasped, but made Himself nothing" (Phil. 2:6–7) and "though He was rich, yet for our sakes He became poor, so that we through His poverty might become rich" (2 Cor. 8:9). How many times have these awful and idolatrous vices not disgraced and continue to disgrace many clergymen, causing them to dramatically lose face and minimizing the validity of their teachings and admonitions? I will refrain from listing the other dangers of the carnal sins, which a priest ought to keep a vigilant watch over so as to avoid, and guard himself, keeping his hands, feet, and eyes under strict obedience. He must especially exercise iron handed control over his inner thoughts and recollections, from which any and all of our actions proceed and take form. These dangers alone, which arise from our old inner self, the bottomless and foul well that each of us bears inside ourselves, would be enough to cause even the most zealous and enthusiastic person to have doubts over whether he should assume the duties of the priestly office. Against these, he who has already received the grace of priesthood and must now lead the others down the road to salvation, is obliged to struggle vigilantly and ceaselessly.

However, in addition to these internal shoals, the ship of priestly ministry must navigate through external reefs, which are equally great and treacherous, and for which he must offer equal care and undivided attention. What are these? They can be found right in the midst of his Christian flock. The life and actions of a priest are always being scrutinized by others. This arises predominantly from man's natural tendency to spend more time preoccupied with the lives and affairs of others, rather than searching and studying his own self. Moreover, when someone is led by an inner motive of love or enmity toward others, then it is with greater satisfaction that he proceeds in gossiping and criticizing, and more easily loses sight and distances himself from the truth, showing that he lacks appropriate judgment of people and things. In his defense of his flight to Pontus, Saint Gregory the Theologian very correctly observes in a most psychologically insightful way that "nothing is so pleasant to men as talking of other people's business, especially under the influence of affection or hatred, which often almost entirely blinds us to the truth" (NPNF[2] 7:205; PG 35:408). If people are generally strict in their judgments regarding others, they are much stricter and harsher in their criticism and evaluations of the clergy. For they do not take into consideration that a priest also "lies in illness" and is subject to human weakness and imperfections. Rather, most correctly and justly taking into consideration his calling and the stature of his divine and superhuman ministry, and demanding of him accordingly, they proceed to attack him without inhibition or the least bit of restraint when he falls. "And all men are ready to pass judgment on the priest as if he was not a being clothed with flesh, or one who inherited a human nature, but like an angel, and emancipated from every species of infirmity" (NPNF[1] 9:52; PG 48:651), St. John Chrysostom writes. How is it possible for a clergyman not to give cause for such bitter comments and harsh criticism? Of course, his first order of business should be to perform his priestly duties with fear and awe, and to diligently see that he does not fall into transgressions of word or deed. We members of the clergy have to admit that in most instances our Christian flock condemns or sharply criticizes us because we give them just cause to do so. On the other hand, each one of us knows and can verify from experience that clergymen who are watchful and vigilant of their actions and words, and who walk and interact with their fellow Christians with discretion and prudence, are excluded from condemnation and accusations made by others. However, as much as a priest may try to exercise care in his daily interactions with his flock, there is always room and cause for him to remember St. Paul the Apostle's advice to Timothy that we cited in the previous chapter: "Pay attention to yourself." Many times, people mistake or misconstrue even the most innocent behaviors, sincere dispositions, and unsuspecting words on our part. This is why we ought to be careful in what we say, what we do, how we walk, how we dress, how we eat and drink, the places we frequent, how we speak, how we laugh, whom we visit, whom we avoid, and all our actions in general, never forgetting that every overreaction and every oversight on our part is capable of drawing unfavorable comments against our sacred ministry, and by extension, impeding the salvation of our flock's souls and the glorification of God. Furthermore, we may find people whom we believe are well disposed to us to be among those scrutinizing and reprimanding us. For this reason, the golden-tongued saint of our Church makes the following excellent and very correct observation: "For all who surround him are ready to smite and overthrow him: not only enemies and adversaries, but many even of those who profess friendship" (NPNF[1] 9:52; PG 48:650).

Having these innumerable dangers in mind, the divine Apostle Paul writes to the Corinthians, "I came to you in weakness and fear, and with much trembling" (1 Cor. 2:3), referring to the internal spiritual concern and care for the success of his sacred mission among the Corinthians. He who "has become all things to all men so that by all possible means [he] might save some" (1 Cor. 9:22) asks the following, with complete assurance of the effectiveness of his labors as a missionary: "Who is weak, and I do not feel weak? Who is led into sin, and I do not inwardly burn?" (1 Cor. 11:29). He advised his beloved disciple Timothy the following, which is worthy of close and continuous study by us clergymen: "Set an example for the believers in speech, in life, in love, in faith, and in purity . . . devote yourself to the public reading of Scripture, to preaching, and to teaching. Do not neglect your gift, which was given you through a prophetic message when the body of elders laid their hands on you. Be diligent in these matters; give yourself wholly to them, so that everyone may see your progress. Watch your life and doctrine closely. Persevere in them, because if you do, you will save both yourself and your hearers" (1 Tim. 4:12–16). St. John Chrysostom was wary and fearful of the same internal and external dangers, and resorted to a trick whereby his friend St. Basil was ordained, but he remained outside the priesthood for a period of time. In speaking with his newly ordained friend, he described in singular detail and with adroitness the difficulties that a clergyman must face at every moment, focusing on the greatest risk that he runs, which is failing in his sacred mission and thus leading the souls of the faithful entrusted to him by God into perdition. It is with great grace and literary beauty that he illustrates this danger and the great responsibilities of a clergyman in the following picture, which he paints for us in his third oration in *On the Priesthood.* "Moreover, if any one in charge of a full-sized merchant ship, full of rowers, and laden with a costly freight, were to station me at the helm and bid me cross the Aegean or the Tyrrhene sea, I should recoil from the proposal at once: and if any one asked me why? I should say, Lest I should sink the ship . . . But where the shipwrecked are destined to fall, not into the ocean, but into the abyss of fire . . . shall I incur your wrath and hate because I did not plunge headlong into so great an evil?" (NPNF[1] 9:49; PG 48:645).

Now, let us examine the means by which a priest will try to enrich and ceaselessly strengthen his inner life, so that he may confront the dangers that lie in wait everywhere against his sacred ministry, and come out victorious.

CHAPTER 3

Prayer

The first and most important medium with which a priest will manage to hold on to his spirituality and create an air of sanctity about him is prayer. Through it a priest can always keep alive his bond with God and revitalize the spirituality that ought to exude from his life. "If you deprive yourself of prayer, you will do as though you had taken a fish out of water: as life is water for a fish, so is prayer for you," St. John Chrysostom says. As soon as he overlooks or feels a sense of indifference toward prayer, his bond with God is loosened, and his life becomes commonplace and mundane, like that of ordinary wage workers, whom he is supposed to uplift and inspire. Spiritual degeneration begins to make its way into his heart. The absence of prayer—the indifference toward this fundamental duty of our spiritual being—is the greatest evil, one that causes the Church inestimable harm and obstructs the fulfillment of its destiny, which is the prevalence of the Kingdom of God on earth. Everyone who does not pray is lacking in spiritual life. But a priest who considers prayer to be some sort of leisure or secondary activity is lacking all the more and fails in his pursuits, utterly ruining himself. "Hatred, discord, jealousy, fits of rage, selfish ambition, factions, envy," and the like, which characterize a good number of us, can be attributed without question to the absence of prayer. These are the fruits of an empty, slothful, idle life that is not uplifted through prayer. On the other hand, the fruit of the spirit, which is also the fruit of prayer, is "love, joy, peace, patience, kindness, goodness, faithfulness, gentleness, and self-control" (Gal. 5:22). But let us listen to the words of St. Gregory of Nyssa, a high-flying master of theology: "Prayer is the guardian of prudence, the seal of virginity, a control of temper, a way to rid ourselves of vanity; it makes us forget our injuries, overcomes envy, and gives us security in peace." A saint of the Western Church writes that "the priest who prays gains gentleness in his manner and external life. From this gentleness proceed luminance and a cleansing of the mind. Such a priest has simplicity and love in his soul when preaching, when leading souls, when preparing people to face death; and this leads the other people to believe that this priest speaks not of himself, but conveys the thoughts that he has been informed of and receives from God Himself." Truly, throughout our priestly lives, we are not only obliged to bear with bravery the disappointment and adversity that affect us directly, but to become angels of comfort and supporters to our spiritual children in the hardships they face. Our very calling and position in society demand that we comfort those in mourning, strengthen those in fear, encourage those who are disappointed, give hope to the unfortunate, and ultimately become all things to all people, in the words of St. Paul the Apostle. Could it ever be possible for us to rely simply on our weak powers to fulfill such a difficult and multifaceted ministry, which demands courage, endurance, and unshakable faith in the Lord? Ought we not revitalize the Divine Grace we received when we entered into the clergy through regular prayer that proceeds from the depths of our very existence, if we want to be faithful and irreproachable servants, and "God's fellow workers?" Let us study our Model—our Lord and Savior, Whom we ought to emulate throughout our lives—in this respect as well. The victory that he claimed at Golgotha was won in Gethsemane. It was there that he came face to face with death by crucifixion, and all the anguish that went along with it. It was there that His human nature shuddered at the martyrdom that awaited Him. For this reason, "He fell on his face and prayed," as one of the evangelists writes, "and He withdrew from them about a stone's throw, and knelt down and prayed," as another also writes. His human nature was highlighted by prayer. He then headed undaunted toward Golgotha, as a conqueror heading toward a triumphant victory.

Priestly work that is not bolstered by private prayer is more than just futile. The idea that we save time by cutting out prayer from our daily activities is a woeful deceit. Perhaps we do in fact save time. But we cut off the spiritual wings with which prayer provides us, and we plunge ourselves into the performance of our daily priestly duties without any inspiration, without that sense of the sublime that is transmitted when we come into contact with the divine. We are changed into common day laborers who mechanically carry out the duties assigned to them. On the other hand, half an hour of daily prayer leaves the seal of sanctity upon us and our soul. It serves as the finest driving force behind every form of speech, idea, or action in our dealings with our Christian flock, and reminds us all throughout the day that we are servants of God, and that we must be in the world without being of the world, and finally that it is our imperative duty to be a living example and model of virtue for those around us. In saying this, it is not my intention either to reprove or teach any of my brothers in Christ. Past experience and the knowledge that I have gained has taught me how much priestly service that is not invigorated by fervent prayer is lacking, and how much it can progress and grow with prayer that is performed regularly and with ardor.

CHAPTER 4

The Reading of Scripture and Spiritually Beneficial Books

Another means through which a priest can succeed in preserving a high level of spirituality, which must characterize his inner life, is to study Scripture, along with other spiritually beneficial books. The Holy Writings are able to make us wise unto salvation, in the words of St. Paul the Apostle. It is one thing to study the Scriptures in order to prepare a sermon, and another to study them for our moral education and the revitalizing of the grace that lies within us. The first instance can in no way substitute for the second, whereas the latter is of great assistance and to the former and facilitates its goals. When we turn to Scripture to seek out passages that are appropriate for our sermons or serve as the basis for a religious discussion that we may possibly want to take up with people who display doubt or indifference, we receive no benefit whatsoever from our studies. We gather knowledge, we study the books that make up the Scriptures, but we ourselves are not edified. "The readings and studies of appropriate edificational books serve to further pique our interest in the good and the divine will, so long as they do not proceed from other interests, nor relate to some other purpose, such as acquiring knowledge in language, history, archaeology, and other such sciences. These studies should be conducted for our own edification in devotion and virtue," writes the wise former professor of the Theological School in Halki V. Antoniadis (*Ἠθική*, vol.

2, p. 76). Moreover, without the habit of studying the scriptures for our own inspiration and the invigorating and uplifting of our spirituality, our sermons will be listless and ineffective, and our persuasiveness in conversations through which we seek to win over doubters or unbelievers and set them on the way of Christ will be lifeless and insipid.

On the contrary, the daily reading of certain passages from scripture in the morning or evening constitutes a necessary and most appropriate form of spiritual nourishment for our soul. "Just as the earth cannot give off wheat if it is not watered, even if it is planted with myriads of seeds, so too will a soul not have any fruit to show even if one were to pour myriads of words into it, if it is not illuminated beforehand by the Divine Scriptures," St. John Chrysostom says. On his oration on Athanasius the Great, St. Gregory of Nazianzus notes that "from meditating on every book of the Old and New Testament, with a depth such as none else has applied even to one of them, he grew rich in contemplation, rich in splendor of life, combining them in wondrous sort by that golden bond which few can weave; using life as the guide of contemplation, contemplation as the seal of life" (NPNF[2] 7:270–71; PG 35:1088).

By the same token, how great indeed is the strength that a priest draws in the performance of his duties from also reading other books of an ethical, ascetic, and generally edifying nature! I sincerely praise the ministers of the churches and denominations of the west as I see the plethora of books of such a nature printed in abundance and made affordable to priests.

In addition, their weekly moral/religious publications always dedicate special sections where they review worthwhile edificational books. In this way, a priest has no difficulty enriching his library with such editions.

However, Greek-speaking priests who wish to delight in such readings and studies can also satisfy their hunger. The ever-memorable Archimandrite Eusebius Matthopoulos' work *The Destiny of Man*, for example, is a book that would be avidly read in the west if made available. The simplicity with which the most sublime truths of our faith are laid out, together with the author's passionate faith in the Savior and His sacrificial work, fill the reader's soul with hope and confidence, and make this one-of-a-kind work most worthwhile. By divine grace, the brotherhood that he founded and led, made up of clergymen and laypersons of virtue equal to his own, publishes numerous books for priests, books that are useful and necessary. To these we can add the majority of the works written by the renowned scholar and clergyman K. Kallinikos. It would completely sidetrack us if I were to list them all, as they are known to almost every clergyman and practicing layperson. A most well recommended book is Thomas à Kempis' *The Imitation of Christ*. Unfortunately, the Greek translation of this wonderful work, done with inexcusable carelessness, deprives the Greek reader of an excellent edificational book. No less worthwhile for edificational reading are D. Mavrokordatos' *θρησκευτικαὶ μελέται* [Religious Studies], translated from German; the orations and speeches of Nikiforos Theotokis, Elias Miniatis, Konstantinos Oikonomos ex Oikonomon; and all the contents of the regular editions of the Greek moral/religious press.

For us clergymen, the writings of the Church Fathers and teachers are excellent edificational books as well. These house the treasures of knowledge of the divine science; and the brilliant and remarkable lessons of faith, hope, and love, which no length of time can alter or diminish. It is truly saddening that the great expenses associated with purchasing the current volumes of the writings of the Church Fathers and their limited editions make these priceless treasures hard to obtain for the Orthodox clergy and people.

CHAPTER 5

Confession and Spiritual Askesis

The priest who places great emphasis on his spirituality will not overlook the need to confess his transgressions. Because we demand—and very justly and rightly so—of our Christian flock that they not overlook the sacrament of Confession, which is of tremendous importance to each and every Christian, it is we who should first set the example for this as well. "It is necessary for those entrusted with dispensing God's sacraments to confess their sins," the ascetic and godly hierarch from Cappadocia notes somewhere. Some time ago, while hearing someone's confession, I was asked, "Since you priests insist so much on the issue of confession, do you confess your sins as well?" In other words, Christians are aware that even after the descent of the Holy Spirit upon them, priests do not cease being human, surrounded by weakness and subject to the temptations of this world; and Christians are of the opinion that priests too ought to confess their sins.

In the Anglican and Roman Catholic Churches, confession for priests is a general rule. Each priest sets aside a period of time annually or every two years to go on a spiritual retreat, which is highlighted by the priest offering his confession. Aside from priests renowned for their spirituality and lengthy experience in Church ministry, priests seeking seclusion or wishing to confess their sins also seek refuge in monastic brotherhoods, which have been set up, among other things, to hear the confessions of clergymen serving in the outside world. Frequently, entire groups of priests are received at their monastic brotherhoods, and having confessed, they examine together the spiritual difficulties that they come across in the world. Each priest speaks about the experiences he has gained and the methods he employs to achieve self-improvement and progress in his work in the parish. Through prayers and hymns to the Lord, they experience a rebirth in the spiritual life, so to speak, and each one of them returns to his place of service with newfound strength, zest, and high spirits. In recent years especially, the Anglican Catholic sect of the Anglican Church has proceeded with even greater intensity to create and systematically form spiritual retreat centers like the ones mentioned above, where priests can engage in self-examination in solitude and prayer. Conferences are held toward this end, and books are written demonstrating the usefulness of these centers of spiritual life and outlining methods to better organize them. These centers provide inestimable benefit to the Church. They revitalize its spiritual powers and provide reserves to its army in the form of soldiers of the kingdom of God, inspired and strengthened "in the grace that is in Christ Jesus."

From what is known to us, a similar work is being undertaken here by the "Zoe" Brotherhood. It would prove most useful to the Church of Greece if the Holy Synod would set aside certain monasteries toward this end, so priests serving in parishes may make their confessions and engage in spiritual *askesis*. A work of this sort would help renew the zeal of priests in a most profound way, while parishes would be the first to feel the beneficial effects of this decision adopted by the Church of Greece. This sort of *askesis* and spiritual self-examination, combined with the sacrament of Confession that will be taking place, will breathe new life into the parish fighting the moral and spiritual battle. It will enable the parish priest to see his mission from a truly spiritual standpoint. It will develop and cultivate the bond in Christ shared by the priests of various parishes, so that they may view one another as brothers in spirit and fellow soldiers in the struggle against sin. Finally, it will present an image of the entire Church covered in an air of brilliance and strength, which neither financial security nor any other measure seeking to serve the worldly aspects of the Church and its ministers is able to accomplish.

CHAPTER 6

Study

At this point, it is appropriate that a few fitting words be said about study, to which a priest ought to devote a set amount of time, so that he may maintain his theological and general knowledge up to par. Being completely cognizant of his mission in the work, the priest must not remain satisfied with the higher or secondary education that he received before entering the clergy. Rather, he should consider it an essential duty to always keep his theological and secular knowledge fresh, and to increase it by studying theological works and following the daily press, along with periodicals related to his work. One of the evils that plagues the Church today is the ignorance of young and old alike on matters related to the faith. Our Christian flock does not know what they believe in and why they believe it. For this reason, many of them are gradually drifting away from the Church and becoming cold and indifferent. The knowledge around us is growing and multiplying. The systems of subversion that are plaguing modern society teach, preach, publish, promote, and disseminate their corrosive teachings abundantly in all directions. Will we remain idle in the face of such conditions, and will we just sit back and come to terms with our enemy at the cost of immeasurable harm to the souls of our spiritual children? Just like other scientists and scholars, we too have a duty to be knowledgeable in the divine science and to follow every movement that takes place therein.

Therefore, the contemporary parish priest must know the dogmatic truths of Orthodoxy. He must try to always keep informed of the main events in our Church's history at the very least, and to enrich his mind with all the apologetic views with which he will defend against and refute the objections and arguments of those who question the truths of Christianity and the Orthodox Church, whenever the need arises. Above all, he will study the scriptures, on the basis of the interpretations of the Church Fathers or some newer treatise, or commentaries written in Greek or a foreign language. He will acquaint himself with their contents very well so that he can draw on their infinite treasures easily and without a second thought, whether teaching or conversing with others, for their edification.

In his posthumously published book on Apostolos Makrakis, the ever-memorable Archbishop Chrysostomos Papadopoulos of Athens writes, "The meticulous study of the Holy Bible and his continuous absorption with it led to his development, and continuously invigorated his theological powers. Undoubtedly, Makrakis owes the greater part of his spiritual and moral standing to the fact that he ceaselessly and meticulously occupied himself with the study and interpretation of the Scriptures in the midst of myriads of other issues and problems" (*Απόστολος Μακράκης* [Apostolos Makrakis] [Athens, 1939], p. 124).

In regards to the above, perhaps there will be some who will say *non possumus* ("we cannot"), citing a lack of time, as some of my brothers in Christ may contend. "These things are not for us, who are struggling to make a living and facing difficult circumstances. Besides, our work in the parish is so multifaceted and strenuous. It is not possible for us to devote time to all these things, which are easy for someone to list from the comfort of his office, where he sits and lays out plans of grandiose ministry and priestly work on lumps of lifeless paper."

However, these contentions are altogether unfounded. Our work is of course spiritual with regard to man's immortal soul. Nevertheless, I believe it is possible to draw a comparison between this work and those called to serve it, and other professions that serve the needs of the common man and his momentary interests. I ask you: Could it ever be possible for a doctor, lawyer, public servant, merchant, or laborer to justify some inadequacy in the profession of his calling by citing the lack of time needed to gain the skill required of him? Surely, the only thing he could expect in such an event would be to go out of business. But, if all these people whom we cited work night and day and willingly undertake every pain to better provide their services and improve themselves in their professions, consider then how many more labors a minister of the Church should undertake, being that he must care not only for the physical well-being and the material interests of those entrusted to him, but for their very spiritual health, salvation, and eternal beatitude. "For what profit is it to a man if he gains the whole world, and loses his own soul? Or what will a man give in exchange for his soul?" (Matt. 16:26). The clergyman who is zealous and faithful to his mission always finds the time to enrich his knowledge.

Besides, from the moment that one has entered the clergy and has placed his hand upon the plough to sow the seeds of the Gospel, he has a duty and responsibility to constantly supplement his knowledge base, adding new information and constantly renewing his existing knowledge, so that he may protect his spiritual flock, not become the subject of ridicule, and most importantly escape condemnation by God on the terrible day when each person will be rendered according to his deeds. Here is what St. John Chrysostom has to say on this matter: "For this reason also, the Lord counsels the man who wishes to build a tower, not to lay the foundation before he has taken his own ability to build into account, lest he should give the passers-by innumerable opportunities of mocking at him. But in his case the penalty only consists in becoming a laughing-stock; while in that before us the punishment is that of fire unquenchable, and of an undying worm, gnashing of teeth, outer darkness, and being cut asunder, and having a portion with the hypocrites" (NPNF[1] 9:64; PG 48:665). Elsewhere he offers the following beautiful words: "There is nothing so prejudicial to the oversight of the Church as this inactivity and negligence . . . For he who is accustomed to enjoy such great freedom from business, and to pass his time in much repose, even if he be of a noble nature, is confused by his inexperience, and is disturbed, and his inactivity deprives him of no small part of his natural ability. But when, besides, he is of slow intellect, and ignorant also of these severe trials, he will carry on this ministry which he has received no better than a statue" (NPNF[1] 9:78; PG 48:683).

We ought to "tend to the people of God with knowledge," as St. Basil says. St. Gregory the Theologian adds, "Accordingly, to undertake the training of others before being sufficiently trained oneself, and to learn, as men say, the potter's art on a wine-jar, that is, to practice ourselves in piety at the expense of others' souls seems to me to be excessive folly or excessive rashness—folly, if we are not even aware of our own ignorance; rashness, if in spite of this knowledge we venture on the task" (NPNF[2] 7:214).

I conclude this part of the book dealing with the priest's inner life by citing the meaningful words in chap. 39 of the Wisdom of Sirach (Ecclesiasticus), which offer us the image of a wise man according to God—someone who ought to be emulated by a minister of the Most High: "But he who gives his mind to the law of the Most High and is occupied in the meditation thereof will seek out the wisdom of all the ancients and be occupied in prophecies . . . He will seek out the secrets of grave sentences and be conversant in dark parables. He will give his heart to resort early to the Lord that made him, and will pray before the Most High, and will open his mouth in prayer, and make supplication for his sins. When the great Lord wills, he shall be filled with the spirit of understanding: he shall pour out wise sentences and give thanks unto the Lord in his prayer."

PART 2

THE EDUCATIONAL WORK OF A PRIEST

CHAPTER 1

The Importance of Preaching

Despite the fact that a priest is chiefly and preeminently a "steward of the mysteries of God," and his purely sacerdotal work—in other words, the priestly part of his ministry—is his most important work, I propose that we examine his work as a teacher, because in reality the former presupposes the latter. The disciples in Ephesus who are mentioned in Acts 19:1–5 were only baptized "into the name of the Lord Jesus . . . [and] spoke in tongues and prophesied" after St. Paul preached to them of Jesus Christ. Before that they had "not even heard that there is a Holy Spirit." St. Paul himself links faith and, accordingly, the display of it—a life in Christ—to preaching. "How, then, can they call on the one they have not believed in? And how can they believe in the one of whom they have not heard? And how can they hear without someone preaching to them? . . . Consequently, faith comes from hearing the message, and the message is heard through the word of Christ" (Rom. 10:14, 17). Therefore, in light of the fact that the existence, growth, and edification of faith all depend in large part upon the preaching of God's Word, it is evident that the priest who does not preach is lacking in the performance of his ministry and is found wanting according to both the Holy Bible and Sacred Tradition.

"Priests speak tenderly to Jerusalem, and proclaim to her . . . You who bring good tidings to Zion, go up on a high mountain. You who bring good tidings to Jerusalem, lift up your voice with a shout," says the resounding Prophet Isaiah (40:2, 9). Our Lord fulfills His earthly destiny preaching and teaching in the synagogues, in homes, by the sea, from the boat, and from the mountain. He directs His message to the multitudes, individuals, His disciples, rulers and private citizens, men and women alike. His disciples, following the example of their Divine Teacher, preach the word everywhere, and in this way were able to cast aside obstacles, overcome difficulties, and change "crooked roads into straight ones, and rough ways into smooth ones." Thanks to preaching, they managed to raise the banner of Christ even upon the palaces of the Roman emperors who persecuted the Christians. The Acts of the Apostles is a narration of their missionary work, and it provides more than a few models for sermons, which the apostles delivered in various instances. The godly Apostle of the Nations, St. Paul, places the greatest emphasis on the importance of preaching, through his words to his disciple Timothy: "Preach the Word; be prepared in season and out of season; correct, rebuke, and encourage—with great patience and careful instruction" (2 Tim. 4:2). Giving an account of his personal work as a teacher and preacher of the Gospel, he writes to the elders of the Church in Ephesus: "You know that I have not hesitated to preach anything that would be helpful to you, but have taught you publicly and from house to house . . . For I have not hesitated to proclaim to you the whole will of God . . . So be on your guard! Remember that for three years I never stopped warning each of you night and day with tears" (Acts 20:20, 27, 31).

The work of the great teachers of the Church and preachers of the Gospel is known to all. Most of their books are made up of sermons that they delivered to the Christian faithful, whom they shepherded in fear, mindful of the account that they will give. St. John Chrysostom—the greatest of ecclesiastical and secular orators—preached almost daily during his eighteen years of service as a presbyter in Antioch and bishop in Constantinople. He continually corrected, rebuked, and encouraged, as St. Paul writes. And he left behind a singular legacy as an ecumenical teacher, as well as rhetorical masterpieces that are truly an immortal and insurmountable perpetual endowment to men of intellect and religion.

If we were to summarize the life of the Church in the East and West from the onset of Christendom until today, we would see that every movement aimed at stimulating and invigorating religious sentiment was as a general rule always accompanied by divinely inspired and vivid preaching, which kindled and touched the hearts of men, and came from the souls of preachers who were absolutely certain of the divine truth they were preaching, speaking in the spirit and strength of the Prophet Elias.

Truly, preaching is a necessary requirement for the existence of a Christian life not limited to drab and pointless mundane procedures, external forms of worship, and outward confessions of faith. We can say that the lack of preaching is a clear example of the lack of apostolic zeal and divine enthusiasm on behalf of the pastors of the Church, and a lack of a genuine Christian life on behalf of the faithful. Preaching instructs the people about what to believe and how to act. It rekindles religious sentiment. It directs the will toward works of altruism and love, and creates from among the Christian faithful sterling examples of the power of faith, examples that exercise great strength in helping to leaven the whole lump of the body of the Church. Preaching is a necessity for people of all social classes, walks of life, and stages of spiritual development in order to bring about their repentance, return, supplications for edification, and salvation. Describing the work of a preacher, St. John Chrysostom underscores the multifaceted goals of preaching: "Wherefore it should be our ambition that the Word of Christ dwell in us richly. For it is not for one kind of battle only that we have to be prepared. This warfare is manifold, and is engaged with a great variety of enemies; neither do all these use the same weapons, nor do they practice the same method of attack; and he who has to join battle with all, must needs know the artifices of all, and be at once both archer and slinger, captain and general, in the ranks and in command, on foot and on horseback, in sea-fight and in siege" (NPNF[1] 9:65; PG 48:666). Likewise, he adds that "the Priest should do all that in him lies, to gain this means of strength," referring to his powers of oration (NPNF[1] 9:65; PG 48:668). A Church devoid of sermons is condemned to a state of apparent death or hibernation, which is obviously detrimental to the shepherds and the flock. A Church that does not give the appropriate attention to preaching and does not enlighten its people through it creates masses of blind superstitious folk who adore procedure, and who end up becoming the cause of scandal, moral depravity, and even crimes—as the centuries-old history of the Church has shown. Precisely due to the importance of the sacred practice of preaching, St. Paul tells the Corinthians in his letter, "For if I preach the gospel, I have nothing to boast of, for I am under compulsion," and he follows with the all-important phrase "For woe is me if I do not preach the gospel" (1 Cor. 9:16).

CHAPTER 2

The Difficulties of Preaching

As stated above, preaching is essential to repentance, return, edification, and supplication, and all these ought to lead to the final goal: the salvation of mankind. From this it is evident that the content of a sermon will vary on each occasion. If we also take into consideration that the congregation to which we are speaking also varies—as it is made up young and old people, men and women, rich and poor, educated and illiterate, devout and indifferent persons—and the circumstances under which we deliver a sermon also differ, it is easy for one to comprehend the difficulties that accompany the practice of preaching the good word. If a priest wants to be successful in the sermons he delivers, he must keep in mind the aforementioned difficulties related to the people to whom he is preaching and the circumstances under which he is preaching. I will elucidate by citing examples.

Say, for instance, one must deliver a sermon in a parish situated in an agricultural or working-class area, where the environment is simple and the people are uneducated and uncultivated. If a preacher uses difficult and grandiose language, with high-minded ideas that are foreign and incomprehensible to the mental abilities of the audience, then his words, their meanings, and the powerful arguments he makes will fly like stray bullets over the heads of the indifferent audience—which is by then yawning and ready to fall asleep—which will be relieved at the sight of the preacher coming down from the pulpit. On the other hand, say someone is invited to preach before an audience of people who are well educated and advanced in the faith, and he uses a vocabulary filled with images and meanings intended for listeners who need to be taught the basic elements of the faith and who are unable to rise above the usual standard sermon. Or say that one must speak to the youth or children who were taught devotion to God by their mothers from infancy, displaying a simple and unfeigned faith, and he begins his sermon by describing the arguments of those who do not believe in a personal God and deny the historic existence of Jesus Christ, so that he can then bombard them with academically rooted counterarguments or complex syllogisms that are difficult to follow. Or say he is invited to speak to an audience of dignitaries who look down upon him and hold the Church he represents—its stature and substance—in low regard, and he opens his mouth to speak from a piece of scratch paper with phrases and points scribbled here and there, holding no unity or order among them. Or say he appears before a congregation longing and thirsting for the word of God, and instead of spreading peace and spiritual comfort in a humble and gentle manner, he shakes his fist in the air, yells, paces ceaselessly, and commits countless other theatrical improprieties. In all these and other such related instances, the sermon will fail to meet its objective, so long as it depends upon a preacher who acts accordingly. If there are some people—few and far between—who appear to be influenced by such a sermon, this is due to the enlightenment of Divine Grace, which always heals that which is infirm, and whose all-powerful strength is completed in our weakness.

On account of these difficulties, which always accompany preaching the good word, a minister of the Church ought to undertake this work with care, suitable preparation for each situation, knowledge of the needs of his flock, and empathy for their possible shortcomings.

It is not my intent to proceed into the details of the theory behind preaching. This is the job of homiletics. I will limit myself to listing certain practical guidelines, after a few words about the necessity of preaching in today's world.

CHAPTER 3

The Necessity of Preaching Today

Today, more than ever, there is a dire need for preaching. Of course, a large majority of Greek Orthodox Christians are religious. Even for those who consider themselves completely indifferent to the faith, there comes a time when they raise their hands up to God in prayer and they externalize feelings of devotion that were passed on to them from devout parents, who upheld the traditions of our fathers and our ancestral faith. Nor, by the grace of God, are there in Greece the millions of folks that one finds in the West who are lacking any religion at all and have never had any relation to the Church whatsoever. They are hostile to the clergy, and enter into holy matrimony or leave this life without the prayers and blessings of the Church, and deprive their young offspring of the necessary guarantee of salvation in Christ: Holy Baptism. Despite everything that is written and said by certain pessimists who exaggerate exceedingly and are used to seeing everything from a negative perspective, Greek Orthodox Christians are devout, and their religious sentiment would be in better shape if they were taught the truths of the Orthodox faith in an organized and meticulous manner. Unfortunately, they are lagging behind in this aspect, but through no fault of their own.

Consider, for example, the ignorance that exists even among the well-educated concerning the sacrament of the Holy Eucharist and its salvific properties and effects, or the significance of the other sacrament that is so closely linked with the Holy Eucharist - Holy Confession— regarding the redemption of our souls, and the fact that in many parts of the Orthodox world it has fallen into a state of inactivity and obsoleteness through our own carelessness. But do we not see this same ignorance in regard to the other truths of Christianity among our fellow Christians, so many of whom have become susceptible to superstitions and unfounded fears. It is no wonder that the devious and immoral practice of Uniatism, as well as other Protestant, and Jewish-leaning propaganda, has found room in which to grow in Orthodox Greece. Sparing no expense in order to achieve their unholy goals, which they set out to accomplish with diabolical fanaticism and obstinacy, the proponents of these ideas ceaselessly spread their misguided beliefs by word of mouth and through pamphlets, and their proselytizing organizations manage to set up bases and posts everywhere, from where they launch desperate initiatives to gain followers and take over territories. If there is not an increase in educational sermons and the already existing ones are not systematized and improved, if we do not produce priests who will engage in teaching in every city and village and who will consider it their absolute duty to preach the word of God in public and private, religious divisions will spring up among us as well, like the ones that are scourging other countries, and the once practically religiously uniform people of our country will become divided. "And every city or house divided against itself shall not stand" (Matt. 12:25).

But the need for preaching today is advisable for another reason no less significant than the former. In today's world, religious affairs are of interest to intellectuals everywhere. Particularly in Europe, major media groups regularly examine the major issues regarding the creation of the world, the destiny of mankind, life after death, and finally the very person of our Savior, Who is at the same time both divine and human. Interest in religious affairs has begun to spread to our local media as well, from which one would hope that Greek Orthodox Christians would receive the proper guidance. However, there lies in our journalists' eagerness to copy their colleagues in the Old and New Worlds a great danger regarding the health and standing of the religious sentiment of Greek Orthodox Christians. The reason for this is the all-too-common phenomenon of our daily newspapers and other media printing even the most irreverent texts that spring from the wild imagination of foreign writers, in their attempt to make a profit out of the latter's ability to write. This results in the falsification and adulteration of the elementary dogmas of Christianity, which have been maintained pure and unharmed by the Orthodox Church.

For the plenitude of the Church, publications of this sort are bitter wells, filled with putridity, which Orthodox Christians are asked to draw from and drink, to quench the thirst they feel for the truths that attract them so. We should not have the expectation that our Christian flock will seek out dogmatic treatises and books written by experts for study and enlightenment. People struggling to make a living and earn their daily bread, who must think day and night about how they will be able to face the difficulties of life, which become harsher by the day, certainly cannot dedicate the necessary amount of time—even if they had it—for serious study. Newspapers are the only source of intellectual pleasure for most of these people. If they find articles and studies printed there, like the ones described above, it is not difficult for one to surmise the damage and destruction that their religious sentiment will suffer. Therefore, there is nothing else to be done but for the faithful to be guided by the teachings of their parish priest. He is the one who is charged with teaching, enlightening, and leading the people from the pulpit, and in all other instances and opportunities.

However, the need for preaching today is also important for the religious development of the youth. In this instance, though, the sermon must take the form of catechetical teaching—a subject that will be discussed in greater detail in the corresponding section.

Still, those who are rooted in the faith and know from tradition and/or personal diligence about our beliefs and how we ought to act have just as much need for teaching to strengthen, advance, and perfect them in virtue. For how can one say that once his thirst has been quenched, he will no longer require water, or that once one's hunger has been satisfied, he has no more need of food? Preaching holds precisely the same significance for man's spiritual life. This is exactly the reason why St. John Chrysostom likens a minister of the Church to a deep running river, whose waters flow ceaselessly. In the same way, he says, that the waters of the river are abundant—whether those that thirst draw water from it or not—so too a minister of the Church ought to always preach, whether those who are listening are many or few. Elsewhere the same Church Father insists on the need for a clergyman to continuously teach his spiritual flock: "Whence it is necessary for the teacher to sow every day (so to speak), in order that by its frequency at least, the word of doctrine may be able to be grasped by those who hear" (NPNF[1] 9:76; PG 48:680).

CHAPTER 4

The Purpose of Preaching

The purpose of preaching is the same one as the purpose that the Incarnate Son and Word of God had in coming to the world, and the same as the one sought by the Church He established. The purpose behind our Lord Jesus' Incarnation was the salvation of mankind and the passing on of the inheritance of eternal life and beatitude to humanity. "I came that they may have life, and have it abundantly" (John 10:10). "I did not come to judge the world, but to save the world" (John 12:47). But at the same time, the Savior's purpose was to glorify God the Father, who sent Him: "I glorified You on the earth, having accomplished the work which You have given Me to do" (John 17:4). "My food is to do the will of Him who sent Me and to accomplish His work" (John 4:34). Meanwhile, the Church that has been established by Christ continues His work—that is, the sanctification and salvation of the faithful—and the success of this mission coincides with the glorification of God. "Let your light shine before men in such a way that they may see your good works, and glorify your Father who is in heaven" (Matt. 5:16). "All these different matters have one end in view, the glory of God, and the edifying of the Church," says St. John Chrysostom (NPNF[1] 9:77; PG 48:682). Therefore, the purpose of preaching is the salvation of mankind and the glory of God.

This end is attained by fighting against sin, which destroys our souls. It plots against the salvation of man, and is as a result ever hostile toward the glory of God. Being that a portion of the population has already been reborn by Holy

Baptism and has entered into Christ's fold, and that there are still others who lie dormant in the darkness of ignorance and have not yet come to know the one and only true God and Jesus Christ who was sent by Him, the purpose of preaching is the advancement, perfection, sanctification, and ultimate salvation of the former and the awakening of the latter by enlightening them with the light of the true knowledge of God that will lead them to Christ, who is the bearer of "Grace and Truth." In the first instance, we have edificational preaching, whereas in the second we have what is known as missionary preaching. It goes without saying that the latter is used for non-Christians and those who have not been baptized, as well as for those who have been baptized but who have lost their sense of morality due to the many sins they have committed and their straying from the Church and its sanctifying office. As a result, they have grown cold through and through, they have "denied the faith and are worse than the infidels." At this point, we proceed to issues relating to the preacher and his sermons.

CHAPTER 5

The Preacher

(a) ***Inner conviction*** – A priest ought to be the first to feel the truths of which he is preaching, as this is the only way that he can speak with conviction and his words may bear abundant fruit. In order to lead others to repentance, we ourselves must have repented beforehand. In order to make others citizens of the Kingdom of God, we must first have renounced every base, self-centered, and materialistic motive, and become faithful servants of Christ the King. Preaching that is done simply for professional reasons and that does not proceed from the very heart of the priest who is teaching his flock will not bear fruit. In this case, what St. Gregory the Theologian describes is applicable: "All are teachers, instead of, as the promise says, taught of God, and all prophesy, so that 'even Saul is among the prophets,' according to the ancient history and proverb" (St. Gregory the Theologian, *Oration 2: In Defence of His Flight to Pontus*, § 8, in NPNF[2] 7:206). Eloquence, rhetorical ornament, an extensive vocabulary, and intricate speech designs cannot make up for the lack of inner conviction on the part of the preacher. The conviction that the preacher feels yields strength of speech, no matter how simple the vocabulary, the style of preaching, or the ideas presented. This strength is transmitted to the audience, which locks on to the speaker and hangs from his every word, thus lending the preacher their full attention from beginning to end.

On the contrary, a lack of conviction creates a spirit of disheartenment in the preacher first and foremost, and the audience somehow instinctively senses his moral weakness and becomes disinterested and disinclined toward the sermon. Many of us are all too familiar with this, having experienced the harsh reality of this truth. Has there never been an instance when, out of duty and need, we took the floor to conduct our work as teachers without prayer, spiritual preparation, and worse of all, bearing the burden of a guilty conscience over some offense in our priestly life? Did we not then hear something like a sort of inner voice blaming and admonishing us? "Doctor, heal yourself first. Priest of God, woe to you for undertaking to teach your people in this sort of spiritual aberration. You had better come down from this sacred pulpit and stand among those who are repenting. This position does not belong to you. You are not worthy of it," the voice tells us. This priest's sermon is lost in the wind. Whereas a priest's unworthiness in no way lessens the power and potency of the sacrament he is celebrating, on the contrary, when it comes to preaching the divine word, this very unworthiness makes the sermon lifeless and dead, "a noisy gong or a clanging cymbal."

Woe, woe, and thrice woe to the priest whose state of spiritual disarray becomes known to the congregation! It is then a thousand times better that he keep silent. If a priest's life does not shine like a beacon and stand as a perpetual sermon speaking in the midst of his flock, if he is not the first to lead a life in Christ and the first to apply the principles of the gospel, he ought not to attempt to teach these things to others. A priest must keep in mind that he has a duty to be "a prophet mighty in deed" (Luke 24:19). The conviction with which a priest will preach will arise from the moral perfection of his person, and will also arise from the understanding that he is preaching a teaching that was invented not by him, but by Jesus Christ, and Him crucified. This conviction was what inspired St. Paul to write to the Corinthians that "I was with you in weakness and in fear and in much trembling, and my message and my preaching were not in persuasive words of wisdom, but in demonstration of the Spirit and of power" (1 Cor. 2:3–4).

The fact that a preacher's personality and the conviction with which he preaches are the most important factors in the success of a sermon are clearly attested to by the example of our Lord, as well as the examples of the apostles and the holy teachers and fathers of the Church. If concerning Jesus Christ, even those who opposed Him admitted that "never has a man spoken the way this man speaks" (John 7:46); if while He taught and boldly rebuked the hypocritical ruler of the synagogue, "all His opponents were being humiliated; and the entire crowd was rejoicing over all the glorious things being done by Him" (Luke 13:17); and if "the crowds were amazed at His teaching" (Matt. 7:28), then these things occurred because our Lord "was teaching them as one having authority, and not as their scribes" (Matt. 7:29), and because He convinced the listeners not by proofs mainly, but "through His personage, which radiated the truth" (*On the Priesthood*, Ch. Papadopoulos, p. 76). The same can be said of the apostles and holy fathers and teachers of the Church. If we conduct a review of those who worthily preach the word of God today, we will see that they speak successfully and effectively, they display strength in their work, and through their virtuous life and overwhelming personality they have become "sweet-sounding instruments fitting to both God and man."

The ever-memorable Dionysios Farazoulis, who used to gather a huge following of laypeople—drawing crowds by the thousands from all corners of Athens and Piraeus, who would hasten like thirsty deer to hear his sermons—owed his success primarily to his unrivaled personality. There were others who were far superior to him in knowledge, wisdom, and rhetorical eloquence, but even the sum total of all these assets could not match the magnitude of his personality, which left a mark all its own in the history of preaching in the Church of Greece.

A priest will speak with conviction and will be a celebrated figure in his own private life and in the eyes of his flock if his inner life mirrors that described in the corresponding section of this book.

(b) ***With every boldness and sympathy*** – There are two extremes in delivering sermons that a preacher of the Divine Word ought to diligently try and avoid: excessive leniency, which reaches the level of serving the weaknesses of the congregation; and excessive austerity, which ends up turning into cruelty.

The former brings disgrace to the pulpit, which rose to a position of prominence not to serve human weakness, but for instruction, which is to be conducted with every boldness. The latter causes even greater stubbornness among sinners and leads them away from places of prayer and preaching. Both result in the spiritual destruction of our Christian flock. When exercising his instructional work, a priest ought to follow the middle ground, the "royal road," so that he does not speak to showcase his talents or out of smugness, but instead proceeds to correct and treat the shortcomings and lapses of his spiritual children with care.

A preacher ought to always keep in mind that he is called by God to make His will known to the people and, furthermore, that he must emulate the holy men of the Old Testament—the prophets—who rebuked the irreverent and sinful people with courage and bravery, warning them of the inevitable divine punishment that awaits. He must emulate St. John the Forerunner, who boldly rebuked the lecherous Herod, and he must never muffle the voice of his conscience in the face of sin.

The great teachers of the Church serve as excellent examples of courageousness and boldness in the service of preaching.

It would not be out of place to cite a few passages from their exceptional writings, which better illustrate the above description. This ought to be the characteristic feature of a sermon delivered with boldness.

In his *Oration 17, To the Frightened Citizens of Nazianzus and the Irate Prefect*, St. Gregory the Theologian writes, "And what of you, the representatives of power and authority? My remarks are directed now to you. We do not wish to appear in any way partial by lecturing the others on proper behavior while giving you a wide berth because of your powerful station, as though we were so obsequious—or terrified—that we waive our Christian right to speak out . . . it is from him [Christ] that you receive your sword, not to use, but to brandish . . . respect your archetype; ally yourself with God, not the ruler of this world; with the good Lord, not the harsh tyrant . . . as for you, man of God, remember whose creature you are and the task to which you are called; how many things you have received and the extent of your obligation; from whom come your reason, your law, your prophets; your very knowledge of God; your absence of despair for the future" (in *St. Gregory of Nazianzus: Select Orations*, trans. Martha Vinson, The Fathers of the Church [Washington, DC: Catholic University of America Press, 2003], 91–92).

St. John Chrysostom's words are equally amazing for their boldness, when in his *Homily 82 on the Gospel of Matthew* the divine father rebukes those who approach the sacrament of the Holy Eucharist without any prior preparation, and admonishes the priests who distribute the Holy Sacraments to such people: "These things I say to you that receive, and to you that minister. For it is necessary to address myself to you also, that you may with much care distribute the gifts there. There is no small punishment for you, if being conscious of any wickedness in any man, you allow him to partake of this table. 'His blood shall be required at your hands.' . . . For this end God has honored you with this honor, that you should discern these things. This is your office, this your safety, this your whole crown, not that you should go about clothed in a white and shining vestment . . . Let no one communicate who is not of the disciples. Let no Judas receive, lest he suffer the fate of Judas . . . Give not a sword instead of meat. Nay, though it be from ignorance that he come to communicate, forbid him, be not afraid . . . But if you dare not to do it yourself, bring him to me; I will not allow any to dare do these things. I would give up my life rather than impart of the Lord's blood to the unworthy; and will shed my own blood rather than impart of such awful blood contrary to what is meet" (NPNF[1] 10:477).

Consider the strength and courage that characterizes the sermon he gave before he went into exile. "Numerous are the waves, and great the tossing of the sea, but we have no fear of going down, for we stand upon the rock. Let the ocean rage as it will, it is powerless to break the rock. Let the waves roll, they cannot sink the bark of Jesus. Tell me, what should we fear? Death? To me to live is Christ and to die gain. Is it exile perchance? The earth is the Lord's, and the fullness of it. Is it confiscation of property? We brought nothing with us into the world, and it is clear that we can take nothing away with us . . . You may fight her [the Church], you will not be able to harm the object of your attack. But whilst you make me more illustrious, you are undermining your own strength by fighting against me. It is hard for you to kick against a sharp goad. You do not take the edge off it, but you make your own feet bloody . . . There is nothing more powerful than the Church, man; give up fighting her, lest she overpower your strength. Wage not war against heaven. If you fight a man, you conquer or are conquered. But if you fight the Church, you cannot conquer. For God is stronger than all."

The prominent seventeenth-century French preacher Massillion, invited to court by King Louis XIV to preach, displayed superb boldness right from his very first sermon. At the time, King Louis was at the height of his power and glory, and was admired by all of Europe. His subjects adored him, everyone adulated him, and he was lavished with all kinds of honors and countless displays of obedience and respect. Massillion's theme was "Blessed are those who mourn," and he used this idea to deliver a sermon that remains a masterpiece and model of ecclesiastical eloquence, as well as boldness and courage from a Christian pastor. He started off his sermon by saying, "Sire, if the people could speak to Your Highness at this moment, they would not address you with the beatitude 'Blessed are those who mourn.' On the contrary, they would say, 'Blessed is the prince, who is always victorious in his struggles, who has filled the universe with his name, who has splendidly enjoyed everything that people admire throughout the duration of his long and successful reign—the grandeur of his victories and triumphs, the love of his people, the respect of his enemies, the wisdom of his laws.' But Sire, the Gospel does not speak as people do. It says, 'Blessed is he who is not the object of admiration of this age, but he who makes the age to come the object of his study, and lives life with disdain for himself and all the things of the earth, for the kingdom of heaven is his.' Not he whose reign and works history will immortalize and enshrine in the memory of the people, but he whose tears will wipe away his sins from history and from the very memory of God Himself, for he shall be comforted."

It is hardly necessary to point out that prominent figures and holy men—bastions of virtue and sanctity—have the license to use this kind of language. However, a priest who is a preacher—especially if he is a beginner—ought to be extremely careful and make sure that he does not end up becoming boring and ridiculous in his attempt to emulate the great examples of master preachers. The admonitions that he will proceed to make during his sermons will depend on his age, the length of his tenure in the parish where he preaches, and his relationship with his parishioners. As time goes by and he gets to know his flock better, and in turn becomes more familiar to them, he will gain knowledge of the quality of each of their characters, and then he may make use of various kinds of allusions, which when performed adroitly and skillfully, will be able to heal inadequacies easier than a forceful reproach delivered in a head-on attack, which only serves to harden those who are on the receiving end. I once heard a preacher speaking, and although I was unable to figure out the theme of his sermon, what I did understand well and remember up until this day—despite the fact that so many years have gone by—was that the preacher had gotten so worked up that he began to attack the luxury sought by women and the waste of money that accompanies it. This attack was strong and direct, and the initiator launched a biting diatribe against his presumed enemy, including threats and terms that were generally just a bit shy of being considered libelous.

All these things were being said in an extremely loud voice, with gestures so exaggerated and numerous that the poor preacher's vocal cords were bordering on exhaustion before he even finished the sermon. His forehead was filled with perspiration, and his entire body was undoubtedly drenched as well. The most tragic thing about the whole story was that the audience began to grow markedly smaller throughout the duration of the sermon. Men and women began leaving, one after the other, some unable to hide their feelings of anger from their faces, others wryly smirking. The sermon had failed. The following words of St. John Chrysostom are fitting for this sort of a preacher: "How then could anyone bear such disgrace as to find that all are mute when he is preaching, and think that they are oppressed, and wait for the end of the sermon, as for some release from work" (NPNF[1] 9:73; PG 48:678).

On the other hand, as the teacher of his spiritual flock, a priest ought to direct his effort toward this end. His entire behavior and lifestyle during his interactions with his parishioners ought to be such that there is complete confidence on their part that every observation made by their spiritual father arises out of love, paternal care, and empathy. In the same sermon cited above, St. John Chrysostom, speaking prior to his exile, and offering an example of singular bravery in the face of Empress Eudoxia and his other persecutors, who were filled with jealousy and evil, gives an example of empathy and care for his beloved people of Byzantium. Here is what he says about them: "For where you are, there I am. We are one body, the body is not separated from its head; Though locally separated, we are in spirit united; even death cannot separate us. For though my body die, my soul will live and be mindful of my people. You are my fellow citizens, my fathers, my brothers, my sons, my limbs, my body. You are my light, sweeter to me than the visible light. For what can the rays of the sun bestow on me that is comparable to your love? The sun's light is useful in my earthly life, but your love is fashioning a crown for me in the life to come."

Both these qualities—courage on the one hand, and empathy on the other—are excellently laid out by St. Paul the Apostle, when in his Letter to the Thessalonians he writes, "We were bold in our God to speak to you the gospel of God in much conflict . . . so we speak, not as pleasing men, but God who tests our hearts. For neither at any time did we use flattering words, as you know, nor a cloak for covetousness—God *is* witness. Nor did we seek glory from men . . . But we were gentle among you, just as a nursing *mother* cherishes her own children. So, affectionately longing for you, we were well pleased to impart to you not only the gospel of God, but also our own lives, because you had become dear to us . . . as you know how we exhorted, and comforted, and charged every one of you, as a father does his own children" (1 Thess. 2:2, 4–8, 11-12).

(c) ***Trained in truth*** – Effective and systematic preaching presupposes as a mandatory condition the training of the speaker in all necessary forms of knowledge, which will give him command of the subject matter on which he will be speaking. Therefore, we ought to be students of those issues that are related to the divine science, to study continuously throughout our lives, and to present the subjects we study skillfully and adroitly. There are many occasions when one grows bored of listening to educated clergyman and wise preachers who did not occupy themselves in organizing and systematizing knowledge that they had drawn on in the past for their sermons. On the other hand, there are others who do not have the patience to study, and try to fulfill their sacred duty as preachers by making use of improvisations and irrelevant ideas. Instead of leading their flock to clean and clear waters that retain their freshness and energy for constant and in-depth study, these people invite them to drink out of diseased waters, which the slothfulness and neglect of the former has caused to become still. The ministry of preaching is so noble and contains such life and strength that it is downright unforgivable when we make it boring and devoid of interest through neglect. A person is fooling himself if he believes that a clergyman who is careless and not studiousness is able to produce edificational preaching, regardless of how imaginative he may be. The product of zero is zero, and ignorance cannot produce anything.

"For since preaching does not come by nature, but by study, suppose a man to reach a high standard of it; this will then forsake him if he does not cultivate his power by constant application and exercise. So that there is greater labor for the wiser than for the unlearned . . . so that whenever anyone excels all others in oratorical powers, then especially of all others does he need laborious study" (NPNF[1] 9:71–72; PG 48:674–75). These golden words spoken by the greatest of ecclesiastical orators is worth studying deeply—especially by those who have gained a decent level of knowledge in the past and remain content with this, always attempting to preach the word of God through improvisation. While they boast that they preach to the congregation by heart, their listeners know all too well just how much boredom they are faced with when listening to their clichés and threadbare arguments.

As mentioned in the first part, the Holy Bible is the first and most important book that a priest ought to study. From it he will receive inspiration, guidance, and enlightenment. It is the richest weapons arsenal from which he will gather his supplies, and he will, "by the armor of righteousness on the right hand and on the left, put on the whole armor of God and enter the arena of combat, to wrestle against principalities, against powers, against the rulers of the darkness of this age."

Scripture is what will give a sermon the necessary ecclesiastical and biblical tone. It is a truly frightful thing to listen to a sermon devoid of any relation to Scripture, which is barely able to be considered and called an ecclesiastical oration.

On the other hand, a preacher must never forget to hold Sacred Tradition as his rule and measure, because he is presenting himself as a teacher of the Church. This will guide him along the road of correctly interpreting Scripture, as well as accurately presenting the teachings of the Orthodox Church.

No less necessary for the training of the teacher/priest are the unrivaled writings of the sacred teachers of the Church, regarding which there has already been adequate mention.

We advise young priests especially, who are burning with the desire to teach their flock, to study the sermons of accomplished preachers. In every other profession, a beginner considers it his duty to study at length the experts of the craft he is about to take up, which he learned in theory at the university or some other school. A novice priest and teacher of the divine word ought to do the exact same thing that a young novice artist, sculptor, musician, surgeon, or lawyer does.

Listening to preachers who have attained the highest degree of distinction is a job especially suited for him, so that he may come to learn in practice the right way to preach. The more preachers he listens to, the better. There is always the danger that if he listens to only one, he may unconsciously end up copying the former's style of preaching, the tone of his voice, and particular phrases that his favorite preacher uses. We must not copy our models, but learn the methods that they employ through diligent study.

On the other hand, those who cannot study alongside living examples due to the location where they are serving can nevertheless study and analyze written sermons that have been published. The study and analysis of a sermon written by an accomplished priest is very helpful. To embark on something like this, one could turn to the sermons of the following persons for study: Elias Miniatis; Konstantinos Oikonomos ex Oikonomon; Michail Glykas; Moschakis; Konstantinos Kallinikos; K. Koidakis, Metropolitan of Plomarion; Michail Galanos; Demetrios Kouimoutsopoulos; as well as the sermons of His Eminence Metropolitan Polykarpos of Gortyna, which are available in leaflets and magazines.

A preacher will draw equal benefit from the fervent preacher P. Trembelas' book entitled *Πρόχειρα ὑποδείγματα ἐκκλησιαστικῆς ῥητορικῆς* [Cursory models of ecclesiastical rhetoric], which is small in size but valuable in content. Also worthy of recommendation are the sketches of speeches published by H.E. Metropolitan Andreas of Triphyllia and Olympia in the journal *Τρεῖς Ἱεράρχαι* [Three Hierarchs], and by Archimandrite Emm. Karpathios in the official publication of the Church of Greece, *Ἐκκλησία* [Church]. Meanwhile, those who speak foreign language have at their disposal a plethora of collections of model orations and sermon outlines. English-language speakers are advised to read the sermons of Newman, Keble, Liddon, Phillips Brooks, Walsham How, Spurgeon, and Melararen, all of which are classic models.

A very interesting and educational exercise is to remove the flesh—so to speak—from an ecclesiastical oration and find the skeleton that gives form and continuity to the entire speech. When doing this, the student must focus his attention on the way in which passages from Scripture and secular literary texts are used, the manner in which parts of the speech and arguments are arranged, and the method in which the preacher begins and ends his speech. We reiterate that the purpose of this exercise is not to use the speeches being studied and analyzed for ourselves, but to learn from them and build ourselves up in the art of preaching. Just like someone who is learning to paint copies of the portraits of Titian, Raphael, or Botticelli to gain skill and training in this art, but who cannot pass off these reproductions as works of his own, similarly, the person studying speeches made by others must not reuse these, pretending to deliver them as his own. This is not the quality of a conscientious person. If an overburdened schedule is used by some to justify breaking this rule of conscientious behavior, the corresponding answer is that in this case it is far better for the priest to read the sermon of another preacher from a book, informing his audience as soon as he begins reading. Besides, the work needed for us to familiarize ourselves with a sermon written by someone else and make it our own in order to deliver it effectively will take the same time and effort—and sometimes more—than what would be required to produce our own sermon.

In general, the priest who wants to dig up old and new gems from the treasure of his heart must always hone and renew his preaching skills through constant study. As busy as he is, he can always find the necessary time to study. Otherwise, despite all the good intentions and enthusiasm he may show at the start of his ministry, his sermons will always end up being led astray into the realm of the platitudinal, and will become boring and meaningless, gradually causing his disappointed audience to grow smaller and leave.

CHAPTER 6

The Sermon

(a) ***Selecting a Theme*** – Now, in order for a priest to deliver his sermon, he must first of course proceed in choosing a topic. This task, as well as the preparation of the sermon, must take place in a timely manner. If the sermon is to be delivered on Sunday, a priest should at least choose his topic by Wednesday, and subsequently prepare and streamline his sermon. Choosing a topic is not as easy as it seems at first glance. In most cases, our sermons are based on the Gospel and Epistle readings of the day. However, the passages from the Gospel and Epistles often contain a plethora of topics that a priest would be able to speak about constructively. It is admittedly difficult for someone to give preference to one of these over the rest. The clergyman who does not serve as a parish priest, but is charged only with preaching the divine word, finds himself in a less favorable position when it comes to choosing a theme. The reason for this is that the better that one knows the Christians whom he will be addressing, and the more spiritual contact he has with them, the easier it is for him to choose the topic of his sermon. A parish priest is the one that enjoys this privilege, being that he is supposed to know his sheep by name and be recognized by them. In either case, choosing a topic will depend on the needs of the congregation. For instance, in a working-class parish, where drinking is widespread, friction and minor arguments between parishioners are commonplace, and the bad habits of gambling, blasphemy, using profanities, and other related behaviors are prevalent, the priest will need to choose topics related to temperance, piety, forbearance, and love.

But a priest has the option—and in fact obligation—not to limit himself to the selected Gospel and Epistle readings, but to discuss topics that are of direct and vital interest to the life of the parish. For instance, he sees that his parishioners do not have adequate knowledge of the great significance that the sacrament of Holy Communion holds. Instead of starting his Sunday sermon as he usually would, speaking about a passage from the Gospel or Epistles, he could begin like this: "Today, my beloved brethren, I want to direct your attention to a very important issue, which relates to our very essence as Christians. From the spiritual contact I enter into with many of my fellow brothers and sisters in Christ during Holy Confession, I have made a very discouraging discovery—many of them do not have adequate knowledge surrounding the sacrament of Holy Communion," and so forth. Starting the sermon this way—which is rather uncommon—will immediately pique the interest of the listeners and cause them to listen to the sermon with all the more attention.

Similar to these are what are known as ***occasional*** sermons, whose choice of topics are delegated by extraordinary events taking place in the parish, the city, or even the country in which the priest is serving.

A priest may also choose to speak on a particular teaching of the Orthodox Church. These sort of sermons, which are of a catechetical nature, are very useful and make a very beneficial contribution. The interpretive explanation of the Divine Liturgy, an analysis of the sacraments of the Orthodox Church, a presentation on Orthodox teaching regarding life after death, the clarification between faith and works, or any of the other truths of the Church can prove very constructive as topics to be developed from the pulpit.

In addition, a series of sermons on the interpretation of a particular book of the Old or New Testament is very advisable because it familiarizes the Christian faithful with the contents of the Scriptures—a knowledge of which the people are sorely lacking.

(b) ***Preparing the Sermon*** – The preparation of the sermon follows immediately after the selection of a topic. As stated above, preparation of a sermon must take place in a timely manner. A work so serious, aiming at moral edification, rebirth, and the salvation of the faithful, ought to be carried out when we are in a relaxed state and not in a rush, when we can devote our full attention and not be hurried, and with contemplation and fervent prayer, not with our mind distracted by all different kinds of mundane daily chores. Besides this, if we proceed in preparing our sermon ahead of time, we will be able to improve parts of it or the entire thing following opportunities that present themselves when we are reading books, receiving visits from parishioners, or communicating with our brother priests, and so forth.

But the most important reason for preparing our sermon ahead of time is the work taking place in us subconsciously. More and more, psychologists are recognizing the significance of the subconscious and the cognitive work taking place inside of us subconsciously and unbeknownst to us. For instance, you read something by one of your favorite authors two or three times in the evening, and when you wake up the next morning you discover that you have memorized the passage you read practically by heart. Your mind was learning it while you were asleep. Or, you are racking your brain trying to solve a problem or trying to remember a name, you search your memory, and after a while you abandon your fruitless efforts. Suddenly, at some point, when your mind is preoccupied with something else, the answer or the name you were searching for suddenly jumps out before you.

The same things hold true with preaching. As a general rule, when you prepare a sermon ahead of time, you deliver it better, more completely, and in a more constructive way than a sermon that is put together on the fly, the night before it is to be delivered. The reason for this is that between the time it is written and delivered, the sermon is augmented, changed for the better, and learned in a more complete way by the priest. Now imagine the benefits that arise for the preacher and listeners when an entire series of sermons is prepared ahead of time. Just consider the perfection that will characterize a series of sermons for all the Sundays in Great Lent, for instance, if a priest chooses the topics for all those Sundays during his leisure time three or four weeks prior to the start of this period of spiritual labors, designs the outlines of his sermons, and gradually works on completing them by adding flesh to the already existing skeleton. In the entire time from the start of his work to the delivery of the sermons, their various parts will be in the priest's mind, where they will be processed and improved subconsciously with every opportunity. When the time comes, the priest will go up to the pulpit and deliver them with ease, but also with great power.

The preparation of a sermon includes finding the saying that will be used to start off the speech and allude to the topic that will serve as the subject of the oration. Next, the introduction, which will proceed from the adage, will allow the speaker to refer to the points that he will develop. The introduction will be linked to the body of the speech, as the head is to the torso. The body of the speech will follow the introduction with a transition that will take place in a natural and unforced way. It will contain arguments that follow upon one another and are presented not suddenly, but instead calmly, like the streams that flow into the bed of a deep river. The conclusion includes a summary of the arguments; an appeal to the pathos of the listeners, whereby the main idea of the sermon will be exalted fittingly; and the closing, which must always be filled with hope and manifest the love and mercy of God for sinners.

(c) ***Delivering the Sermon*** – In order for the priest to deliver his sermon, the question arises as to what is the best way for this to be done: from a manuscript; based on notes that include several details in addition to an outline; or without any notes at all, recited completely by heart. First and foremost, it must be stated that regardless of the manner in which the sermon is delivered, it must be fully written out. From the moment of his ordination and for several years after that, a priest ought to write out his sermons and not leave out even the smallest detail. When he is able to acquire satisfactory ease following the lengthy experience he has gained, then—in the event that duties that cannot be postponed arise—he may preach based on detailed notes that cover the entire sermon.

There exists among us a bias against delivering a written sermon from a manuscript. On the contrary, in other countries this method of delivering a sermon is considered completely natural and does not cause the slightest scandal to the consciences of the faithful. In England, for instance, priests deliver their sermons from a manuscript as a rule. Prominent British preachers like Liddon and Spurgeon read their sermon aloud word for word.

Canon J. G. Simpson from St. Paul's Church in London is considered to be the finest contemporary preacher in England, and he always writes and reads his sermons in this manner. Therefore, there is nothing wrong with reading a sermon out loud, nor is it a sign of inferiority.

All of us, however, more or less know from experience that when we work to prepare our sermon, memorizing it is but a matter of short time. Some preachers, who are in the final stages of having conscientiously prepared their sermon, are in a position to recite it by heart without any difficulty. There is likely no priest out there who is unable to memorize a sermon that he wrote and read over carefully four or five times. The memorization of a sermon allows for an inspired delivery. For those out there who do not have faith in their memorization skills, they may draw up an outline of their manuscript on a piece of paper and bring it with them as they speak from the pulpit.

When the priest delivers his sermon, he ought to keep in mind that the decency and sanctity of the pulpit leaves no room for inappropriate displays of anger and loud screaming that leaves behind a bad image. Novice preachers in particular seem to believe that they can prevail upon the audience and draw the attention of the congregation by raising their voice. The speaker is better off resembling a deep river whose waters flow calmly and grandly, changing desolate areas into fertile fields, rather than torrential rapids rushing with a thunderous rumbling, causing only damage and destruction. A demeanor that is calm and majestic, manifesting the solemnity and spiritual aestheticism of the preacher, leaves an effect even on those who were not intent on listening to the sermon when they first entered the church.

Too many erratic gestures distract the attention of the audience instead of helping them to focus. Gestures—as few as possible and carefully planned out—should be presented more as a form of natural expression and a way of emphasizing the point of the words. "The middle tone of voice is to be preferred, neither so soft as to elude the ears, nor so loud and strong as to be vulgar" (Basil the Great, *Letter 2*, § 5, in *Saint Basil: The Letters*, trans. Roy J. Deferrari, Loeb Classic Library [London: William Heinemann, 1926], 18; original in PG 32:229).

PART 3

THE PRIEST AND CHILDREN

CHAPTER 1

What Goes On Elsewhere

In Roman Catholic and Protestant countries, as well as in England, religious instruction—especially the catechetical preparation of children—is numbered among a priest's duties. Every parish priest has a responsibility to teach children the fundamental truths of the Church in which they were born and baptized, because prior to their confirmation, which will take place somewhere between the ages eleven to fourteen, they must take a test to determine how much knowledge they possess regarding the major tenets of the Church to which they belong. Only then will they receive their confirmation from the hands of the bishop.

The Book of Common Prayer in the Anglican Church has a special section regarding the catechesis of children called: "A Catechism, that is to say, an instruction to be learned of every child before he be brought to be confirmed of the bishop." In this chapter, questions and answers are used to present the Apostles' Creed, the Lord's Prayer, the Ten Commandments, and the two sacraments—Baptism and the Supper of the Lord—that the Anglican Church officially recognizes to have been instituted in the Church. According to this chapter on catechism, as soon as the children can say in their mother tongue the Articles of Faith, the Lord's Prayer, the Ten Commandments, and can also answer such questions of this sort, they shall be examined by the bishop or his appointee, and they shall then be brought to the bishop by their godparent in witness of their confirmation. The Book of Common Prayer lists the following note at the end of the chapter on catechism: "The Curate of every parish, or some other at his appointment, shall diligently upon Sundays and holy days, half an hour before Evening prayer, openly in the Church instruct and examine so many children of his parish sent unto him, as the time will serve and as he shall think convenient, in some part of this Catechism." Furthermore, in a separate paragraph, parents and masters are urged to send their children, servants, and apprentices to church regularly to receive their catechetical instruction from the priest. Therefore, it is an imperative duty of the priest to attend to the catechism of the youth in the parish where he was sent to serve, in the same manner that it is his duty to hold holy services during the morning and evening. He cannot ignore or overlook the performance of this duty, because when his bishop visits the parish to administer confirmation, the priest undergoes examination together with the children, so to speak, with regard to the fulfillment of his catechetical duties.

However, the parish priest in England, who always has complete scholarly training, is not alone in fulfilling this delicate and extremely responsible duty. Men and women with knowledge of catechism—which they received after attending special seminars given by the Sunday School Union, founded in 1785, five years after the establishment of Sunday Schools took the form of a nationwide movement thanks to the efforts of Robert Raikes—volunteer their services to help the parish priest. In addition to them, he has at his disposal a plethora of books serving as aids, which present in detail instructional methods, content, and an abundance of other useful instructions for the smooth and effective religious instruction of the youth.

CHAPTER 2

What Goes On Here

Unfortunately, we are lagging behind in this aspect. Just a few years ago, catechetical instruction as a parish movement was unknown to us. The family and school were the only parties responsible for the religious upbringing of Greece's youth. The clergy considered their involvement in this affair as foreign to their mission. In fact, there were even people who held positions of prominence within the Church who said this salvific catechetical movement smacked of Protestantism when it first began to appear in certain parishes in the Greek capital. In spite of all this, everyone capable of speaking and writing never tires of repeating and emphasizing that there are three constituents who need to work together in harmony for the religious upbringing of the youth: the family, the school, and the Church.

This begs the question: How can the Church contribute to this work? What do all those who in their writings and speeches highlight the importance of the Church in the religious instruction of the youth mean? Perhaps this will take place or has taken place in the past through church sermons? One would have to be very naive and not know a single thing about the soul of a child in order to make this argument. There is no doubt that the Church can only contribute to the religious edification of the people's children by systematically setting up Sunday Schools in every parish and giving particular attention to special means designed for the cultivation and growth of religious fervor among the youth. During the first years of the appearance and operation of Sunday Schools in

England, Adam Smith had this to say about them: "No plan or means promises to bring about a change in the manner and spiritual development of childhood itself as Sunday School does. This is the most effective means of reaching the above goal since the age of the apostles."

Fortunately, in recent years, we too have begun to develop an appreciation for the usefulness of Sunday Schools. The work of the ever-memorable Fr. Markos Tsaktanis of St. Catherine's Church in Plaka, Athens, received the blessings of the Primate of the Church of Greece, His Beatitude Archbishop Chrysostomos of Athens, while the former was still alive. The archbishop placed this work of the strong and zealous laborer of the gospel under his personal patronage, and following the death of this pioneer of the catechetical movement in Greece, his blessed work was passed on to the equally capable hands and prominent figure of Fr. Angelos Nisiotis, parish priest of the Zoodohos Pege ("Lifegiving Font") Church. Fr. Nisiotis had the zealous Archimandrite P. Kalliontis supporting him in his catechetical work, and managed to draw several thousand young men and women to his community center, his parish, and various other parishes in Athens and Piraeus, where he established and built-up branches of religious instruction. This wonderful social work was supported by the publication *Καινὴ Κτίσις* [New Creation], which was issued by Fr. Angelos' organization and operates with a staff of young women motivated by divine zeal who are guided by their related knowledge in the area and who are led by the leader of this movement and his aide. They are the ones who teach the catechism to the children and instruct them in their religion.

A more standardized catechetical instruction is offered in the Sunday School established under the watchful eye of His Beatitude Metropolitan Chrysostomos of Athens and run by the clergy and lay members of the spiritually fruitful Zoe Brotherhood. According to the official publication of the Church of Greece, "At the end of the year [1929–1930], 12 lower-level Sunday Schools were operating in Athens and Piraeus with teachers from the Zoe Brotherhood, including one monk, three university graduates with a degree in Theology, and eight college graduates. A total of 1,550 students registered throughout the year, and approximately 800 would attend classes regularly . . . Over 100 students were registered throughout the year at the senior Sunday School in Athens. Instruction revolved around developing the basic truths of the faith—not just dogmatically and graphically, but through apologetics as well. Based on the same format of the Sunday Schools operated by the Zoe Brotherhood, over the past year 24 lower-level Sunday Schools were established in various cities around Greece, in addition to five senior schools. So, the total number of these Schools all across the country amounted to 36 lower-level schools and six senior ones, with 4,680 total students registered, and 3,410 who attended classes regularly" (*Ἐκκλησία* [Church], no. 27 [1930], 222). It is with great joy that we hail this auspicious start, and we express the hope that the catechetical movement will spread throughout Greece and include the everyday citizens, because the malleable soul of a child deserves our full attention.

CHAPTER 3

The Soul of a Child

Three very important factors are most correctly considered to be responsible for a child's upbringing: a pious family surrounded by healthy traditions; a school that is cognizant of its lofty mission; and a living Church, which is led by the Holy Spirit. The soul of a child deserves the attention of all three of these. Our Lord pointed to the significance of a child's soul as the quintessential model of innocence and spirituality. "Then Jesus called a little child to Him, set him in the midst of them, and said, 'Assuredly, I say to you, unless you are converted and become as little children, you will by no means enter the kingdom of heaven. Therefore, whoever humbles himself as this little child is the greatest in the kingdom of heaven'" (Matt. 18:2–4). Christ loved children with all His heart and was in turn loved by them. Large numbers of children followed Him into the desert together with the thousands of people, whom He fed with five loaves of bread. Children stood and watched Him enter the Sacred City on Palm Sunday, and exuberantly cried out unto Him "Hosanna" in jubilation. When the chief priests and scribes saw the children crying out in the Temple and saying, "Hosanna," they complained to Jesus. He answered them by saying, "Have you never read, '*Out of the mouth of babes and nursing infants You have perfected praise*'?" (Matt. 21:16). Children instinctively ran toward the Divine Teacher, drawn in by His sweetness and divinity, while the apostles forbade them from approaching. Then Jesus said to them, "'Let the little children come to Me, and do not hinder them, for the kingdom of heaven belongs to such as these'... and He took them up in His arms, laid His hands on them, and blessed them" (Matt. 19:14; Mark 10:16).

A child is a treasure that God entrusts to us. He is a treasury of innocence, living water, a clean well in which the surreal beauty of the spiritual world is reflected. A child is a link uniting humans and angels. Finally, as it is often said, a child is royalty.

For all of these reasons, we ought to afford the greatest respect for the innocent and guileless soul of a child. Each child has been endowed with various powers, which when developed will form his character. A child is not a piece of clay whom parents or teachers or priests are able or even allowed to mold in the manner that they desire and approve of. Furthermore, a child is not some sort of toy, nor a wild animal that is destined to be domesticated through fear and threats.

Each child has a unique personality that needs to grow and develop in a loving environment, with exemplary edification and sanctity, because a child learns more by what he sees than by what he hears. A child's soul may be like wax, so that the examples he witnesses can be ingrained therein, but it becomes tough like marble and rigid when it comes to removing the impressions that have been formed there. A child is like a camera when it comes to forming a perspective of the things taking place around him, and his memory stores and reproduces the impressions ingrained upon his soul—good or bad, healthy or perverse—as if they were on film. So, the upbringing of children ought to be done with religious piety and great care.

CHAPTER 4

Religious Education

The purpose of education is to help children develop normally and complete themselves to the greatest possible degree. This is accomplished through the efforts of the intellect and will. The discipline by and through which these efforts of the intellect and will are led is called "education." However, if the mind ought to exercise itself accordingly so that it may make valid observations regarding life's phenomena and think correctly, if the consciousness needs to be enlightened and strengthened, if the will must be trained so as to always desire the good, in this case the goals of education must be something that does not relate to the pupil's ego, but elevates him above his personal self-interest. It is evident that for a child to receive an education that lives up to its name and will present the child as a useful member of society, he must be educated with the intent of serving others, and of following and fulfilling the will of God. In other words, a child's upbringing must be religious through and through. This is the sole and salvific truth.

Other systems of education that may be presented, by which children are raised into men capable of engaging in trade and increasing their wealth but which overlook religious education, may pique the interest, but they are incapable of laying any claim to the term "education." If by the word "education" we mean the principle one, the one that fits the above definition, from whose respectable laboratories there proceed people who are well balanced, pillars of society, and apostles of healthy ideas, then we cannot but accept that the goal sought by this type of education is of valid importance to the Christian Church, regardless of religious instruction, which nevertheless ought to be a part of it.

With the belief that true education must be inspired by God and have its end in God, we have a fundamental duty to give religious instruction the position it deserves in education. Without it, education will fail in its mission. Religious instruction is a necessary precondition to a religious upbringing. Children need to learn about God, as He was revealed to us by Jesus Christ. It is in Jesus Christ—and only in Him—that they can discover the fullness and completeness of the truth.

CHAPTER 5

Factors in Religious Education

Without a doubt, it is the family that holds the most prominent position in a child's upbringing, which, as stated, ought to be religious. This will lay the foundations upon which the other two pillars will be built. School and Church are no less significant factors in this effort. But when the family ignores its duty, it is not possible for schools or the Church to produce anything of significance. A child who has not learned to offer prayers to God from infancy, from the lap of his mother or father, has suffered inestimable injustice from his parents.

School will fill the gaps left by the family and complete the work it left undone. This is not a matter to be addressed at present, nor is it the goal of this present work to address what ought to be done at school regarding the religious instruction of children. However, we cannot help but point out the sad truth that religious instruction—a *sine qua non* in terms of upbringing—has been pushed aside of late in Greek schools. It is precisely this fact—that upbringing ought to be religious in nature, to be guided by God, and to be rooted in Him—that is being overlooked in favor of curriculums designed by educators who are not familiar with the nature and mentality of the Greek people; who corrupt our sacred national ideals and religious traditions; and who enthusiastically copy foreign systems, which have no relation whatsoever to the special characteristics, nature, and history of the Hellenic Christian world. They believed that everything that takes places elsewhere can be applied in Greek lands. The results are evident and apparent to all. Aside from offering a subpar spiritual and mental preparation, these systems produce students with weak characters, citizens of small stature, and unstable members of society.

It is a fact that for some years now the official Church of Greece especially has been involved in an ongoing struggle to convince the state to give the subject of religion the place that it deserves. Despite the improvements that are set to be enacted or were done so already, the Church maintains its complete responsibility for the religious instruction of Greek Orthodox Christian children. The promising catechetical movement that has recently begun needs to be strengthened, so that it may breathe new life into every part of Greece, and throughout the entire Greek Orthodox world for that matter. Toward this end, catechetical instruction needs to take on a standardized form to ensure that it will bear fruit. Today's priests, who have enjoyed receiving a higher or at least secondary education, as well as all the priests of the future, should automatically be considered as the catechetical instructors of children as soon as they begin their service in the parish.

CHAPTER 6

Establishing and Organizing a Catechetical School

Let us now assume that a newly chosen and ordained priest is burning with zeal to establish a Catechetical School in the Church that he will be assigned to serve in once he begins his priestly career.

Of course, the first thought that comes to mind is how he will attract as many students as possible. In order to succeed in this effort, before he does anything else, he must get parents to become interested in their children's religious instruction, so that they may come to realize the great benefits that their children will gain from catechism and instinctively cooperate with the priest. In order that he may bring parents even closer to this effort and generate even more enthusiasm among them, it would prove useful if he were to invite men and women on two consecutive Sundays interchangeably to the church—or community hall where available—and explain the lofty goals that the newly established Catechetical School will seek to fulfill and serve. At the same time, he should encourage them to consider this work as their own and to support it by regularly sending their young children for catechetical instruction. Finally, he should proceed in electing officers—men and women separately—from among the most well-educated and pious parishioners, so that he may have them as supporters and aides in the work of catechism.

As is always the case, however, not all of them will heed the priest's calling and attend these meetings. For this reason, he will visit those who were absent at their homes and explain to each and every person all that is to be gained from offering religious instruction to the youth. In parishes with a congregation that is somewhat educated and cultivated, a priest may also present his thoughts about the Catechetical School in writing and distribute this document to the homes of his parishioners. Another opportunity during which a priest may speak to his parishioners about the usefulness and benefits of a Catechetical School arises when he visits their homes to perform various prayer services. During this time, instead of engaging in any other fruitless and pointless conversation, he may choose to bring up the topic of the family's spiritual development and the need to care for the religious education of the children, a need that will be excellently served by the Catechetical School.

This kind of systematic effort will surely bear fruit. On the Sunday that will be designated beforehand as the first day of classes for the Catechetical School, children may be accompanied by their parents. Following a brief prayer, the priest may once again speak about the importance of the catechetical work that will be taking place in the church, which will reflect upon the entire parish. In this way, parents are bound, so to speak, by the priest's words, which they are listening to together with their children. The majority of them will assume the responsibility of supporting and aiding the efforts of their parish priest, willingly or unwillingly, at the very least to preserve the standing of parental authority in their eyes of their children.

The work of catechism is chiefly the responsibility of the priest. He is the one who is to be considered the leading figure and driving force behind the catechetical movement taking place in the parish. However, he may train young men and women to aid him in his catechetical work in order to make it easier for him while he handles his other parish duties. These aides to the catechetical instructor/priest—always operating under his leadership and guidance—may hold group meetings with him from time to time to prepare lesson plans for upcoming Sundays. Each aide will assume the instruction and catechetical training of a group of students.

CHAPTER 7

Methodology of Catechetical Instruction

The catechetical instructor ought to proceed in teaching a lesson entirely and not analytically. In other words, he ought to first explain, develop, and clarify the lesson for the students and then direct questions to them. Furthermore, he should not force the students to learn and memorize the material beforehand and then proceed in explaining and clarifying it. The analytical method tires the minds of students, while always yielding poor results.

In explaining the lesson, the catechetical instructor ought to seek not only to enlighten the minds of his students, but to explain the conclusions in a practical manner, filling the students' souls with love for God and the exercise of virtue. In other words, the enlightenment of the mind must go hand in hand with the shaping of the heart. Besides, there are areas of catechism where detailed explanations and proofs ought to be avoided diligently. The priest himself, by virtue of his standing, is guarantee enough of the truth behind his words. Students believe what is being said because the priest is saying it. A presentation of logical and philosophical proofs regarding the existence of God, the divinity of Jesus Christ, and so forth, is complete overkill and in fact scandalous to the minds of the young students.

When teaching, the catechetical instructor ought to speak using language that is simple, clear, and understandable by all. The measure of the language employed will be the students of the lowest level of intellectual development, who take longer to comprehend the lesson's content.

Questions unrelated to the material being taught should be avoided, as well as sarcastic or biting remarks in the event that the student does not correctly answer the question directed by the catechetical instructor. It is better that the instructor first pose the question and subsequently ask for a volunteer who will answer it.

The catechetical instructor must make sure to draw the full attention of the students to what he is saying. This is why he must continually make eye contact with the students while teaching and refrain from moving back and forth or looking down and only casually glancing at them from time to time. If the teacher does not keep his eyes on the students continually, they will lose focus and direct their attention elsewhere, causing the teacher to frequently speak to an inattentive audience, where some students are yawning, others are being unruly, and others are engaged in something similar.

Finally, the catechetical instructor must love the children entrusted to him, discerning in each of the students the guileless and invaluable soul that God the Father created and loves, and for which our Lord Jesus Christ laid down His life. Love, more than anything else, will make the priest capable of understanding the students who receive the catechesis and of being understood by them.

CHAPTER 8

The Catechetical Lesson

In order for the catechetical instructor/priest to now proceed with the catechetical lesson itself, he must be aware of the purpose behind the establishment of a Catechetical School. As mentioned above, the ultimate goal is religious instruction, which is the most important part of the entire educational process, characterized as religious and being so by necessity, in order to "help the children develop normally and complete themselves to the greatest degree possible," based upon the view that the purpose of human life is to fulfill the Divine Will and serve others. The full attention of the catechetical instructor ought to be devoted toward this goal, and he ought to direct all his energies, including the most insignificant action, toward this end.

The entire content of the religious instruction that will be taught to students receiving the catechism can be divided into a four-year curriculum, while students can be placed into one of four different groups. The first group, encompassing students up to the age of seven, will be taught certain aspects from the history of the Old and New Testaments, aspects that facilitate the purpose of catechetical education. Special attention will be given so that when the children are taught the history of the New Testament, they will be sure to learn about the most important miracles performed by the Lord, in order to impress upon their tender souls and ensure that they remember throughout their lives that the founder of our faith is the Omnipotent and Almighty God. The second group, which includes children ages eight to ten, will be taught the catechism, by which we mean not only the beliefs of the Orthodox Church and the actions accompanying them, but elements of liturgical life as well. The third group, including children ages eleven to thirteen, will study certain periods in Church history. The fourth group, composed of students age fourteen and above, will be taught select sections of the New Testament, which, along with it being explained, will be tied in by the catechetical instructor to everything that was taught during the three previous years of study.

At the start of each lesson, the priest will invite the students to pray, and this shall always be accompanied by an ecclesiastical hymn chanted by all the students, who will be led by their catechetical instructor.

Following the prayer, the priest may proceed with announcements related to the students. For instance, he may praise the diligence, order, cleanliness, and decorum of all those who possess these virtues. On the other hand, he may describe the negative consequences of slothfulness, disorderliness, uncleanliness, or audacity in store for all those who are characterized by these flaws, but he should avoid mentioning the names of the students to whom he is referring.

Next, he may proceed in examining the students, keeping his questions as short as possible. Even if the students' answers do not address the question in its entirety or are partially wrong, the instructor should not interject with his own explanation, but should correct the students' response, so as to help them develop their own initiative and lend them courage.

Now, following the review of the previous lesson, the new lesson of the day will be taught. Each lesson given, or at the very least parts of it, must relate to and address issues with which a child is familiar. This is the method followed by our Lord, Who used to speak in parables to the multitudes that followed Him. Besides, children learn by relating new knowledge to previously existing knowledge. The various truths that are taught to the children must be made applicable to everyday life in the world that surrounds the children's souls. Words and phrases that are hard to understand must diligently be avoided.

When giving a new lesson, the catechetical instructor must (a) define the aim of the lesson being given; (b) capture the interest of students through a brief introduction and accompany the new lesson with concepts and images that are known and familiar to them from the past; (c) develop the new lesson in such a way so as to keep the interest of the children high and make them want to memorize it, and immediately ask questions regarding anything that was not understood—the new lesson ought to be presented to the students in a logical order and structure; and (d) make the conclusions applicable to everyday life and relationships, as well as to our responsibilities to ourselves, God, and our neighbor.

In order to make all of the above more specific and understandable, we cite examples of lessons for all four groups into which the students coming to receive catechism will be divided.

(a) EXAMPLES OF LESSONS FOR CHILDREN UP TO THE AGE OF SEVEN:

(i) Abraham and the Three Angels

Aim of the lesson – To demonstrate that God knows the desires and yearnings of our soul and is ready to help us, and to cultivate the virtue of hospitality in the souls of the students.

Introduction – We have said on many occasions that God is our Father, loves us, provides for us, and constantly desires to come to our aid and fulfill the desires of our soul that do not go against His will, do not harm our happiness (understood in the correct sense) or the material and spiritual interests of others, and serve to glorify and magnify Him. All that we need to do is remain faithful to His holy commandments and practice them in our daily life—most importantly love, a manifestation of which is hospitality. So, we shall see how a righteous person who is hospitable and respectful to others receives from God everything that he has been asking of Him for many years.

New lesson – The story of Abraham and Sarah: These two people were devoted, good, and wealthy, but they did not have children of their own. One day, as Abraham was sitting outside of his tent, while Sarah was busy with the housework, he saw three strangers. They seemed tired. Without waiting for them to ask for any hospitality, he invited them to rest under the oak tree that was located near his tent. He offered them water to wash their feet and rushed to bring them meat, butter, and milk. The strangers ate, recovered from the exhaustion of their journey, asked about Sarah, and foretold that she would give birth to a son and thus fulfill the couple's longtime desire. These three strangers were angels of the Lord. Sarah was shocked when she heard this. Abraham, full of joy and ever gracious to the strangers, who he was now convinced were supernatural beings, accompanied them as they prepared to leave. A little while later, the prophecy spoken of by the angels was fulfilled: Sarah and Abraham had a son, and both of them were happy.

Conclusion – God always hears our prayers and fulfills our requests. However, a necessary and chief condition for the fulfillment of our desires is the observation of God's commandments and the display of love, no small part of which is hospitality (Rom. 12:13; Heb. 12:2).

Note – The instructor/priest will draw the students' attention far more effectively if he pitches or draws a tent and explains why people lived as nomads back then and used tents. He can also show the different parts into which a tent was divided, which part belonged to the men and which part to the women, and so forth. The image of a tent, built as a model by the catechetical instructor, will help the students' interest reach its pinnacle and ensure that not even one word from the entire lesson will escape them.

(ii) Paul Resurrects Dorcas

Aim – Today we will learn about the double duty that we have toward our neighbors: to pray and work on their behalf.

Introduction – Prior to His Ascension into heaven, Christ told his disciples, "Go and preach the gospel to all nations." Following their Teacher's instruction, the disciples traveled to cities and villages preaching in the synagogues, markets, town squares, and anywhere else they could.

New lesson – During his travels, Peter entered Joppa, where he met Dorcas, a woman devoted to the teaching of Christ who did many good works. Next, describe her efforts on behalf of the poor, whom she would sew garments for and clothe. She was full of good works. She fell ill and died. The brothers summoned Peter. He prayed and called upon divine intervention to resurrect Dorcas. Make sure to stress the point that Peter emulates Christ (who resurrected Jairus' daughter, Lazarus, and the young son of the widow from Nain), the difference being that Christ acts through His own divine power, whereas Peter prayed to the Lord and entreated Him to use him as an instrument of this divine strength.

Conclusion – God works on behalf of people. He raised Dorcas from the dead through Peter. He clothed the poor through Dorcas. Each one of us can become an instrument of God by praying and working on behalf of our neighbor. Children have a duty to pray for their parents and other people as well, especially their young friends who are in need. They must help them. Let them offer them their small savings, which they may have set aside for the purchase of some unnecessary item.

The catechetical instructor will adhere to this order of operations when teaching the aforementioned content to the four groups into which the students of the Catechetical School will be divided. Keeping in mind this model lesson and the observations and suggestions that preceded it, the catechetical instructor will be able to rather easily develop the initiative to plan the lessons for the catechetical curriculum to be taught throughout the entire year.

(b) EXAMPLES OF LESSONS FOR CHILDREN AGES EIGHT TO TEN

(i) The Sacrament of Holy Communion

Aim – To demonstrate that we as Christians ought to be united with Christ, as branches are to the vine.

Introduction – We have seen in the history of the New Testament that prior to His Passion, Christ instituted the sacrament of Holy Communion at the Last Supper. Ask several of the students what they remember from last year's lessons about the events that took place during the Last Supper. Relate and compare the sacrament of Holy Communion with the other sacraments, and highlight the fact that during this sacrament we receive not only the grace of the Holy Spirit, but our Lord Himself inside of us.

New lesson – Define the sacrament. State who celebrates the sacrament, the materials that are used as gifts, and when the bread and wine are transformed into the Body and Blood of Christ. Talk about the duty of Christians to partake of the sacrament of Holy Communion as often as possible. Discuss the necessary preparation, and so forth.

Conclusion – Emphasize the importance of the sacrament of Holy Communion. He who abstains from it is far from Christ. His soul is deadened, much like the branches that wither when they break away from the vine.

(ii) The Fourth Commandment

Aim – To demonstrate the duty of Christians to rest on the seventh day and keep it holy, just as they must work during the other days of the week.

Introduction – Rest is necessary for physical health and to keep a person robust. Continuous work adversely affects health and lessens the productivity of work. A horse that works constantly without rest becomes exhausted and is rendered useless. An engine that is not taken apart from time to time to be oiled and cleaned loses its strength, and so forth. However, continuous idleness destroys the body and soul.

New lesson – What does the Fourth Commandment teach us? Read the text of the commandment and explain it. Discuss the ways in which we can keep the Sabbath holy: by attending church, through edificational reading, by doing good works for the suffering, by taking trips that rest the body and refine the soul. Explain how the duty of work is understood from the same text of the commandment: "Six days you shall labor and do all your work." Discuss the pitiful outcome of idleness. Work is part of God's law. Cite examples from Christ, the apostles, and the saints. Cite example of great modern-day men of devotion.

Conclusion – In the same way that we have a duty to work, we have been given an equally important duty to rest for the sake of physical and spiritual health.

(c) EXAMPLES OF LESSONS FOR CHILDREN AGES ELEVEN TO THIRTEEN

(i) The Persecutions Against the Church

The following sample lesson can be used to teach students about each individual persecution separately.

Aim – To demonstrate that the Christian faith has a divine origin and is therefore invincible.

Introduction – We know from the history of the New Testament that ever since the onset of Christianity, it has been met with hostility, hatred, and persecution. Christ said this as well: "In the world you will have tribulation."

Talk about Herod and Christ, the scribes and Pharisees, the persecution faced by the apostles, the persecution faced by St. Paul and those in his company, idol worshipers engaged in the systematic persecution of Christians.

New lesson – Describe each of the Roman emperors who persecuted Christians: Nero, Domitian, Trajan, Marcus Aurelius, Septimius Severus, Maximian, Decius, Valerian, and Diocletian. Describe the methods of torture used by each of them. For example, during Nero's reign, Christians were sewn inside the skins of animals and thrown to the wild lions as food. They were also doused with flammable liquid and burned. List the saints who were martyred during each of the persecutions—men and women, clergy and laity. Example: St. Paul the Apostle was martyred during the reign of Nero, and so forth.

Conclusion – The persecutions and their leaders have faded, and Christianity has prevailed. The reason is that Christianity has a divine origin. It is not man-made. The persecution of the Church in the Soviet Union and any other such movement taking place anywhere in the world should not discourage us. In the face of all these challenges, the promise made by the Savior stands out: "Take courage, I have conquered the world."

(ii) St. John Chrysostom

The following is a sample lesson that can be used in teaching the lives of other Church Fathers and teachers, with a few alterations.

Aim – To demonstrate (1) that faith and divine zeal give a Christian stability and make him invincible, (2) and that although Chrysostom was crushed by the weight of human evil, the unwithering crown of glory awaits him in heaven.

Introduction – All the holy martyrs and confessors drew spiritual strength from their unshakable faith in God during their struggles on behalf of Christianity. We had an opportunity to see the heroism of St. Stephen the First Martyr. The divine example offered by the Savior of the world gave them courage. They never retreated in their struggle on behalf of virtue. The power of faith, which can move mountains according to the promise of the Savior, is most excellently exemplified in the lives of the great fathers of the Church.

New lesson – Talk about St. John Chrysostom's parents, his studies, and his upbringing. His passion for Christ and zeal led him to leave behind guaranteed success in the world and turn to the Church. His spent six years studying and praying, withdrawn from the outside world. His health suffered due to the rigors of his lifestyle and his frequent fasting. He returned to Antioch, where he was ordained a deacon and then a presbyter. He became a divinely inspired preacher filled with the fervor of divine zeal. He was elected Patriarch of Constantinople in 398, but he soon clashed with Empress Eudoxia. He was first exiled in 403, but upon his return he unleashed an even stronger attack against the vices of the court. A second exile followed, filled with hardships. He died in Komana, and his final words were “Glory to God for all things.”

Conclusion – Only faith can strengthen us in our efforts on behalf of virtue and the prevalence of divine will. We stand firm in our faith toward God in spite of persecutions, slander, and defamation. If God is with us, who can be against us? If our enemies win out against us by taking positions, titles, and seizing material goods, these things ought not to lead us into temptation and cause us to despair. We have no eternal city here. Our citizenship is in heaven (Heb. 13:14; Phil. 3:20). Chrysostom’s enemies crushed his body, but his memory remains ageless, and he will forever be honored as a saint and confessor, triumphant in heaven along with the other saints.

(d) EXAMPLES OF LESSONS FOR CHILDREN AGES FOURTEEN AND OVER

Luke 15:11–32

Aim – To demonstrate that God is always ready and willing to forgive us, provided that we sincerely repent for our previous life of sin and decide to no longer return to our old ways.

Introduction – Our Lord, as we have said before, made use of parables in order to place greater emphasis on the truths that He wanted to teach, and in order to ensure that the crowds would be able to follow the things He was preaching about more easily and with greater interest. The catechetical instructor should then expound upon what a parable is. Christ left us many parables. One of the nicest—if not *the* nicest—is the Parable of the Prodigal Son.

New lesson – Read, explain, and analyze in detail the text of the parable. The catechetical instructor may ask one or two of the students to read this parable aloud as well. Taking occasion from verse 20, students can be taught about how a house was designed during that time, the importance of a fatted calf (v. 23), the significance of a ring (v. 22), who the older son represents (v. 25), and so forth. The prodigal son returned repentant. Ask the students what they remember from the sacrament of Confession. After welcoming his prodigal son, the father ordered the fatted calf to be slaughtered in his honor. After repenting, the sinner confesses his sins and approaches the spiritual table so that he may partake of the Lamb of God, who was sacrificed on behalf of the life and salvation of the world. Ask the students what they remember regarding the sacrament of the Holy Eucharist. Naturally, it is understood that the content of the parable can go as far as the desire and zeal of the catechetical instructor takes it, by relating it to the prior knowledge acquired during previous years, in addition to other parts of the Gospel, such as the Parable of the Good Shepherd or of the Lost Coin. This topic could easily be divided into two lessons.

Conclusion – God is always ready to forgive us for as many transgressions as we may be guilty of. Repentance is the greatest of all gifts, as is the sacrament associated with it, which our Church teaches and upholds. Through it, we are able to cast away the stain of sin and become sons of God and recipients of His inheritance.

In regard to the teachings of the parables from the Bible, I think that the model lesson cited above is more than enough to ensure complete understanding of the method in which catechetical instruction of select passages from Holy Scripture ought to be conducted. The catechetical instructor will divide the curriculum content matter into units and will apply the method shown above to teach each lesson. Finally, it should be added that every prayer and ecclesiastical hymn ought to first be explained and interpreted, and then be given to the students for memorization, so that whether praying or singing, they may do so with the knowledge of what they are saying.

The above covers the educational duties of a priest. At the point, we proceed to examine his sacerdotal work.

PART 4

THE SACERDOTAL WORK OF A PRIEST

CHAPTER 1

General Observations

The center, basis, and essence of a priest's entire ministry is his sacerdotal work—the celebration of sacraments—through which Divine Grace, which justifies and sanctifies a person, is passed on to the faithful. This is the main job for which a priest is called into his divine service by the Church, and this work stands as the alpha and omega of his mission.

A priest's educational and catechetical efforts aim to prepare souls to accept the sacraments and unite themselves with Christ. These efforts represent the narthex, or shell of the fruit, whereas a priest's sacerdotal work is the actual temple and the nucleus of his entire ministry. Through his educational work, a priest teaches about the need to participate in the sacraments of the Church, the conditions, and the spiritual state required on behalf of those interested in worthily entering into these mysteries, as well as the significance of the rites that encompass and accompany them. Through his sacerdotal work, he passes on to the people these very sacraments, which justify and sanctify them. "Let a man so consider us, as servants of Christ and stewards of the mysteries of God" (1 Cor. 4:1). Through His sacraments, our Lord continues His salvific work on earth through the clergy, even after His glorious Ascension into heaven.

The streams of Divine Grace flow bountifully from these sacraments, as if from a source of water springing into eternal life, upon the plentitude of the Church and upon each of its members. Baptism inducts us into the Church and allows us to be born again. Chrismation strengthens us in the spiritual life, into which we were born through Baptism, and enhances our strength in the struggle against the evil one. The Holy Eucharist sustains spiritual life within us and makes it fervent. Repentance returns us to a state of righteousness and sanctity, from which we may have strayed away and fallen away through sin. Priesthood offers the necessary means of intercession between God and mankind in order to engage Divine Grace. Matrimony sanctifies the union between man and woman for the creation of a family—the sturdy base upon which society is founded. Finally, Holy Unction heals our physical and spiritual infirmities.

Our Lord Himself is the force behind the sacraments, whereas the priest celebrating them is merely His vessel. It is the Lord who baptizes, releases us from our sins, offers Himself as a sacrifice upon the altars of God's holy churches. He is our eternal High Priest "who does not need daily, as those high priests, to offer up sacrifices, first for His own sins and then for the people's sins, for this He did once for all when He offered up Himself" (Heb. 7:27). Because it was not possible for Him to remain with us perpetually in bodily form, He placed priests as His servants and made them participants in His eternal priesthood. "Also, there were many priests, because they were prevented by death from continuing. But He, because He continues forever, has an unchangeable priesthood. Therefore, He is also able to save to the uttermost those who come to God through Him, since He always lives to make intercession for them" (Heb. 7:23–25). Therefore, the priest is not only a representative of Jesus Christ, but in some respects Christ Himself. A priest's strength and office proceed from Christ's crucifixion, and all that they possess belongs to Him.

In light of the significance and mission of the sacraments, it is evident that a priest ought to proceed in celebrating them with respect and awe, following exactly all that the Church has prescribed regarding them.

As is known from the study of Church dogma as well, the fulfillment of the sacraments does not depend on the moral qualities of the priest. Sacraments are valid and fulfilled even in the event that a priest is not up to par with his mission, provided that he has the intent to celebrate the sacraments and uphold the rites prescribed by the Church regarding each one of them. "And there could not have been either baptism, or the body of Christ, or oblation, through such, if in every instance grace required merit. But as it is, God uses to work even by unworthy persons, and in no respect is the grace of baptism damaged by the conduct of the priest: else would the receiver suffer loss," St. John Chrysostom writes (NPNF[1] 12:44).

Although a priest's moral misbehavior does not affect the fulfillment of the sacraments, he is under no less obligation to proceed in celebrating them with pure hands and a clean heart. Through his entrance into the priesthood and the great honor that he has been afforded to celebrate the things "that the angels do not dare look into," he has become a vessel and instrument of the Holy Spirit. Therefore, he must be possessed by fear and awe lest he defile this priceless treasure that he has in clay vessels. He who celebrates the sacraments under the weight of a deadly sin commits sacrilege and a serious offense for which he will have to answer when he appears before the awesome judgment seat of Christ. Being that a priest may be called upon to celebrate a sacrament at any moment and repeatedly, he is compelled to always be ready. For these reasons, he ought to always lead a life that is truly priestly, maintain the robe of sanctity intact and unblemished, and always be united with the supreme and eternal High Priest, our Lord Jesus Christ.

For all these reasons, a priest's inner life and the spiritual environment in which he finds himself and lives must be in keeping with our description in part 1 of this book.

Note – There will not be a discussion regarding the sacraments and the sacerdotal acts of the Church involved in each one of these. As is known, teaching regarding these things is offered in the dogmatics of the Orthodox Church, and liturgics gives a detailed interpretation of all that is read and chanted in the Church during the services of Vespers, Orthros, the Divine Liturgy, the sacraments, and the other sacerdotal services of the Church. The priest should refer to these books to answer any questions or seek clarification. The Church Typikon (book of directives and rubrics) will serve as his sole guide whenever he officiates a service, and he will follow it faithfully and to the letter, avoiding every addition or subtraction not foreseen therein. The Church Typikon houses the centuries-old tradition of the Church. There are members of the faithful who are advanced in the nurture and admonition of the Lord, and through habit and faithfully following church services, they are well aware of every directive in the Typikon. They are exceedingly scandalized and distressed when it comes to their attention that the priest has disregarded the Typikon. Therefore, every condensing or skipping of the long-standing texts read or chanted in church is reprehensible, as it runs directly against the Typikon. Nor is a priest who proceeds in leaving out anything justified in doing so on the argument that he is seeking to lighten the burden of the faithful. If the Church recognized such a right for its ministers, it would have done away with uniformity of services, and the traditions of entire centuries—which the Orthodox Church has preserved as a faithful custodian—would be overturned. If there is anything to be corrected, the sole Church body that is responsible for addressing this is a synod of bishops, not local priests, who are obliged to unwaveringly uphold everything that is prescribed by the Church.

CHAPTER 2

The Church

Now, in order to examine the truly divine work being undertaken by the priest in the Church, it is deemed necessary to make reference to (a) the Church, (b) the priest, and (c) the faithful.

The Church is the chief site for worshiping God, and for this reason it must stand out for its complete cleanliness, orderliness, and beauty. Fortunately, we can say that most of the Orthodox churches in the Church of Greece fully meet the above requirements of cleanliness, orderliness, and beauty. However, there are no small number that testify to all else save the fact that they are the central places for the worship of God. The floors are dirty and filled with stains from oil or other substances that have spilled; the pews are falling apart; and the dust is piling up on the windows, and even on the icons and holy vessels—an equal number of which are damaged and dirty. There are sacred texts with their pages torn or partially eaten by a booklouse, due to their many years on the bookshelf. Other books are simply thrown here and there on the windows located near the chanter's stand. All these things and other similar phenomena indicate neglect or indifference by the priest, the parish council members, and the sexton for the cleanliness and beauty of the holy church. Nevertheless, it should be added that all these inappropriate and unbecoming things observed in churches speak not only of neglect and indifference, but great disrespect shown by all of the aforementioned, who are charged with vigilantly attending to the beautiful appearance of the house of God in all things. Moreover, if one were to consider that none of these responsible parties would stand for such unbecoming and dirty conditions in his private home, we are very justified in terming the dirtiness and disorder seen in some churches as disrespectful and as an absence of a basic fear of God.

If the entire church must stand out for its order and cleanliness, there is all the greater reason why this must be said for the holy sanctuary and the holy altar. Complete order and sparkling cleanliness must characterize both of these areas. The holy altar is the divine area where the Most Holy Sacrament of the Divine Eucharist is celebrated, during which the bread and wine are transformed into the Very Body and Precious Blood of our Lord, God and Savior, Jesus Christ. During this solemn mystery, He who is "enthroned on High with the Father" is invisibly present upon the holy altar in the form of the holy gifts of the bread and wine, and comes to be sacrificed and "give to all the faithful His own self for heavenly food." Similarly, the Body and Blood of our Lord are kept constantly and ceaselessly upon the holy altar to be given to the sick. Therefore, both the holy altar and the table of preparation (or *prothesis*), as well as every other area in the holy sanctuary must appear extremely clean, beautiful, and sparkling for the glory and honor of Him Who in His infinite mercy and condescension to us, His trifling and unworthy servants, stands among us to unite with us in order to sanctify and save us. God, speaking through the Prophet Haggai, says, "The silver is Mine, and the gold is Mine" (Hag. 2:8). There is absolutely no justification whatsoever that is allowed or that stands regarding a so-called lack of resources to maintain sparkling cleanliness and order in the holy sanctuary and the holy altar. Every expense toward making the church in general—but especially the sanctuary and the altar in particular—more dazzling and glorious, so to speak, is completely justified, whereas every observable disorderliness or filthiness in the holy sanctuary is the sole and exclusive fault of the priest. He is the pastor, the leader, the teacher, the celebrant, and therefore he ought not for a moment stand for the slightest unsightliness in the church. Moreover, it has been observed that any instructions given by him regarding these matters are practically followed as a rule by the parish council, which should not be considered as holding the slightest responsibility regarding at least the holy sanctuary and holy altar. The

Lord says through the Prophet Malachi, "Behold, I send My messenger, and he will prepare the way before Me. And the Lord, whom you seek, will suddenly come to His temple" (Mal. 3:1).

CHAPTER 3

The Priest

Inside the church, the priest is not to stand, walk, or sit as he would when he is outside. The church is a holy and sacred place. It is completely and utterly different than every other place. It is the House of God. The Most-High God is worshiped inside the church. The most holy sacrament of the Divine Eucharist is celebrated in the church, along with the other sacraments. The Body and Blood of Christ are constantly housed in the church. For all these very important reasons, a priest ought to enter into the House of God with the fear of God and reverence, and move about, speak, and carry himself therein with deep devotion, humility, and concentration. Sudden movements, disorderly and hurried walking, and loud conversations with chanters or the sexton indicate a lack of comprehension regarding the sanctity and holiness of the area, and must therefore be avoided with extreme care. Afterward, upon following the directives of the Typikon of the Great Church of Christ in order to celebrate the Divine Liturgy, a priest ought to "take the *Kairos*" prior to putting on his holy vestments by prostrating in front of the bishop's throne and then praying at the *soleas* in front of the icon screen, or iconostasis. There is unfortunately no small number of priests who, in addition to other arbitrary innovations, have introduced the practice of skipping the entrance prayers or not "taking *Kairos*," as directed by Church protocol. Instead, they hurriedly enter into the holy sanctuary and, devoid of any piety, proceed to kiss the Gospel book or holy altar, and subsequently proceed to put on their vestments.

However, this amounts to disrespect and disregard for the directives of the Church, which we demand that the laity follow and honor.

Once a priest puts on his vestments, as he recites in a low voice the corresponding verses from the psalms for each vestment he wears, he proceeds to the Holy *Prothesis* (Table of Oblation) to prepare the Holy Gifts—the bread and wine—for the Liturgy, faithfully adhering to the Liturgy of Preparation. The bread must be made from wheat, because it will later be changed into the Body of Christ. Christ compared Himself to wheat when He said, "Truly, truly, I say to you, unless a grain of wheat falls into the earth and dies, it remains alone; but if it dies, it bears much fruit" (John 12:24). The old tradition of the Church attests to this, requiring that the bread being offered for the Holy Eucharist always be made out of wheat. Likewise, the wine must be pure from the grapevine, bearing no other mixtures whatsoever. The reason for this is that this was the wine that the Savior used during the Last Supper, and protocol—as well as the Sacred Tradition of the Church from the first days of Christianity until our time—has called for such a pure and genuine wine from the grapevine to be used. Therefore, the bad habit that exists in certain provinces of Greece that produce resinated wine, where priests use it for the sacrament of Holy Communion, is entirely contrary to Church tradition and order.

The holy chalice and the *diskos*, which will receive the Holy Gifts, as well as the asterisk and holy veils, ought to sparkle with cleanliness. When a priest is God-fearing, he will always want this and will manage to ensure that the vessels in the church will be worthy of the sacred use for which they have been intended. When he wants this, he will convey these feelings to the parish council members, the majority of whom will readily adhere to every correct instruction given by their parish priest. Even if the finances of the parish are limited and resources are lacking, there are always devoted parishioners—both men and women—who consider it a special privilege and sacred blessing to make a contribution on behalf of the holy vessels of the church. Everything depends upon the piety and desire of the priest.

Now, regarding the celebration of the Holy Liturgy, the priest's duty - a holy and utterly imperative one—is to remain fixed in front of the holy altar from the start of the Liturgy until the end, and move only when it is time for the entrances, or to read from the Gospel and bless the people. He may only be seated during the reading of the Epistle. The priest must also teach the parish council members, the sexton, and the altar boys that throughout the duration of the Divine Liturgy, they are not allowed to approach him for any reason whatsoever in order to inform him of anything. There can be no exception to this rule. Every Orthodox priest visiting the church of another denomination, be it Catholic, Anglican, or Protestant, remains shocked by the deep reverence of the clergy, on account of which their priests remain planted in their positions like pillars of salt from the start of the holy service that is being celebrating until the finish. They move only when it is time to sanctify, read the Gospel, and bless the people. Conversations or exchanges between the priest and the parish council members, the sexton, or his servers for issues pertaining even to the church itself or the service—something that takes place in the Holy Sanctuaries of Orthodox Churches very often, or better still as a rule—is unthinkable and practically impossible for clergymen of other denominations. There, everything is addressed ahead of time down to the last detail, and so there is never a need that arises for the priest to interrupt the holy service. Unfortunately, this very thing happens among us, and from this standpoint it is cause for great tears and deep sorrow, as well as repentance on behalf of every priest and bishop. When a priest stands before the holy altar and celebrates the bloodless sacrifice, he ought to be giving his undivided attention and give himself over to deep and heartfelt prayer on behalf of his spiritual flock, on behalf of the living and the departed. It is then when he is chiefly and preeminently the intermediary between God and men, having become such by the transformation he underwent during his ordination, for "while continuing to be in all appearance the man he was before . . . by some unseen power and grace [he has been] transformed in respect of his unseen soul to the higher condition," as St. Gregory of Nyssa says (NPNF² 5:175). During these moments, having become ethereal and bodiless through his supplications for the salvation of his spiritual children and the entire world, a priest's inner being ought not to be drawn away by any other worldly thought. "For as though he were entrusted with the whole world and were himself the father of all men, he draws near to God, beseeching that wars may be extinguished everywhere, that tumults may be quelled; asking for peace and plenty, and a swift deliverance from all the ills that beset each one, publicly and privately," St. John Chrysostom says (NPNF[1] 9:76; PG 48:681). When the Holy Spirit is called upon and the gifts of bread and wine are changed into the very Body and Blood of the Lord, imagine how much attention and inner exaltation, and how much piety, is demanded of the priest. Here are the beautiful thoughts of the very same Church Father on this issue, and they are worth the clergy's undivided attention and complete interest: "At such a time angels stand by the priest; and the whole sanctuary, and the space round about the altar, is filled with the powers of heaven, in honor of Him who lies thereon. For this, indeed, is capable of being proved from the very rites which are being then celebrated. I myself, moreover, have heard someone once relate, that a certain aged, venerable man, accustomed to see revelations, used to tell him, that he being thought worthy of a vision of this kind, at such a time, saw, on a sudden, so far as was possible for him, a multitude of angels, clothed in shining robes, and encircling the altar, and bending down, as one might see soldiers in the presence of their King" (ibid.).

It is toward them that the priest ought to read and speak, clearly and audibly pronouncing the words and phrases that require emphasis, and avoiding any inappropriate hastiness and precipitancy, on account of which a good number of clergymen gradually end up swallowing entire verses and paragraphs, causing great religious harm and scandal to the faithful who hear them and do not understand what they are saying. We read not for ourselves, but for others. And because every reading must be done slowly and not hurriedly, so that the people may understand what is being read, this should be done with all the greater care when it comes to a priest reading holy texts that contain lofty and sacred meanings, and relate to religious edification itself and the salvation of the people through Jesus Christ. St. Paul the Apostle says that "even things without life, whether flute or harp, when they make a sound, unless they make a distinction in the sounds, how will it be known what is piped or played? For if the trumpet makes an uncertain sound, who will prepare for battle? So likewise you, unless you utter by the tongue words easy to understand, how will it be known what is spoken?" (1 Cor. 14:7–9).

Whenever a priest reads prayers and supplications or chants, he ought to avoid undisciplined vociferations or a style that is overly affectatious, because these elements are foreign to the hallowed ground of the church and lead the congregation to believe that the Lord's minister is more interested in filling their ears with his melodic voice than uplifting their souls and raising them above earthly thoughts. Besides this, undisciplined voices distract the congregation and leave a bad impression on the more cultivated members. A priest should always keep in mind Canon 75 of the Sixth Ecumenical Council, of Constantinople (in Trullo), which is included in the Typikon of the Great Church of Christ and instructs as follows: "We will that those whose office it is to sing in the churches do not use undisciplined vociferations, nor force nature to shouting, nor adopt any of those modes which are incongruous and unsuitable for the Church: but that they offer the psalmody to God, who is the observer of secrets, with great attention and compunction. For the Sacred Oracle taught that the Sons of Israel were to be pious" (NPNF[2] 14:398). In interpreting this canon, Zonaras writes that "the chanting, or psalmody, that is done in churches is in the nature of begging God to be appeased for our sins. Whoever begs and prayerfully supplicates must have a humble and contrite manner: but to cry out manifests a manner that is audacious and irreverent. On this account the present Canon commands that those who chant in the churches refrain from forcing their nature to yell, but also from saying anything else that is unsuitable for the church. They are womanish members and warbling (which is the same as saying trills), and an excessive variation or modulation in melodies which inclines toward the songs sung by harlots." Of course, church chanters in particular ought to turn their attention to the above all the more. However, they too take example from and follow all that the presiding priest instructs them to do and the manner in which he conducts the parts of the Divine Liturgy and other sacraments that include hymns.

When called upon to give Holy Communion to a sick person, a priest must hasten to the destination without delay. There are instances in which the sick person suffers from a contagious disease, and other instances in which an outbreak of an infectious disease has spread throughout the parish. Even in these cases—and even if his life is in danger—it is the priest's duty to willingly perform his ultimate duty toward his spiritual children, that is, to give them the Body and Blood of the Lord for the remission of their sins and life eternal, while always keeping in mind the words of the Lord: "The good shepherd gives His life for the sheep . . . the hireling flees because he is a hireling and does not care about the sheep" (John 10:11, 13). During moments like these, Divine Grace, which came upon the priest during his ordination to the ranks of the clergy and accompanies him all the days of his life, comes to his aid and strengthens his weakness. It supports his heart, and he feels such power within himself that he completely ignores danger and death. It is as if the voice of the Holy Spirit whispers in his ear at that moment, "You are Mine . . . When you walk through the fire, you shall not be burned, nor shall the flame scorch you. For I am the Lord your God, the Holy One of Israel, your Savior . . . Fear not, for I am with you" (Isa. 41:1–2, 3, 5). In spite of all this, the priest should make sure to take every precaution to avoid contracting the illness, and he should see to it that he makes use of the precautionary methods and means recommended by science, in order to safeguard his health and life.

CHAPTER 4

The Faithful

The first and most essential duty of a priest in regards to the relationship between the faithful and their Holy Church is to make them love their parish and to unfailingly attend the Divine Liturgy. He must remind them through his sermons, and most importantly through his visits to their homes, of the duty they have to sanctify themselves in the church at least once a week, and explain that the holy fathers instruct that any Christian who is absent from the holy gathering of the Divine Liturgy for three straight Sundays without justification be cut off from the Church. In all the foreign churches and denominations, a pastor considers it his sacred duty to visit the Christian faithful missing from the Sunday gathering at their homes and find out the reason for their absence, as well as to admonish them appropriately so that this mistake is not repeated. If after one or two or three attempts, he is not heeded, those who overlook their essential duty to attend services are removed from the list of the faithful and are considered dead to the Church. Unfortunately, this is not the case with us, and the reason for this is surely the lack of zeal on behalf of the clergy for the salvation of the faithful.

Moreover, a priest must strive to ensure that the Christian faithful not only attend church services, but attend services in a Christian manner. Unfortunately, we all know full well about the disorder that characterizes our churches and the great noise and disarray that is present at the gatherings—which are supposed to be holy—taking place in Orthodox churches, especially during Holy Week.

We have grown accustomed to blaming our beloved Christian brethren for all these unpleasantries; however, we are wrong. We might be justified in laying the blame on them if we previously exhausted all the resources at our disposal to enlighten and instruct them. But if this had taken place, things would be different, as is proven by the instances of the (sadly) few churches in which complete devotion and order prevails from the start of holy services until the finish, due to the zeal, deep devotion, and spirituality of the priest serving there. When the Christian faithful are enlightened appropriately, and most importantly when they are given as a model the devoted conduct of the priest in the church, as well as the behavior of the parish council members and the other church personnel, then sacred silence and tranquility, which ought to distinguish a place of worship, will gradually prevail in all of our churches. Unfortunately, many times, the bad example of noise and idle talk is set in the holy sanctuary and the *Pangari* ("candle stand")—precisely the two parts of the church that are preeminently responsible for maintaining order during holy services.

Of course, one may argue that lengthy services—especially when accompanied by a sermon—are a major reason for the disorderliness that is observed in our churches, and which manifests itself either by many members of the congregation leaving prior to the end of the Divine Liturgy, or through pushing and shoving and conversations arising among the faithful during holy services. Yet, if one visits an Orthodox church in Russia, where even pews and chairs around the church are a foreign element, he will see that thousands of Christians stand at attention throughout the entire duration of Vespers, which is chanted together with the service of the Orthros or the Divine Liturgy and which lasts much longer there than it does in Greek churches. Regardless, however, of this example set by the sister churches in Russia, the number of pews should be increased and the number of chairs multiplied in our churches to provide greater comfort to our people, who as a general rule work so hard to make ends meet, thus allowing them to fulfill their religious duty and facilitating their attendance at church services.

The priest, however, will play a major role in encouraging the faithful to attend services in church, ensure tranquility and sanctity during the Divine Liturgy, and keep the congregation inside the church until the end of holy services if he tries to make the content of the Divine Liturgy and the most common hymns and readings understandable to the parishioners, and if he encourages the congregation to all chant out loud at least some of the most beautiful hymns from our Orthodox worship services. If the people observe the celebration of divine worship in other churches with close attention and deep reverence, this is undoubtedly due to the fact that the language in which the readings and hymns are written is completely understandable to them. A person who comprehends and understands the meaning and importance of what is being sung and read in the church prays in a manner altogether different than a person who does not understand their meaning. In fact, the latter is probably not in a position to pray. Who can deny that not only members of the Christian faithful, but the majority of our priests as well, are not in a position to understand not only most of the passages of the Psalms and the Epistle readings, but many parts of the Divine Liturgy itself, which is so frequently celebrated and repeated, due to their lack of proper instruction? However, there are guidebooks for the Psalms (Marinos, Kallinikos), as well as the Epistle readings (P. Trembelas) and the Divine Liturgy (Panagiotopoulos and others), through the help of which the parish priest will be able to completely understand all that he is chanting and reading and was heretofore unaware of, and as such, be able to help his Christian flock to arrive at the true meaning of these texts. This is when the gains will be the greatest for the spiritual progress of the parish, and all the Christian faithful—excluding of course those who work in body and soul on behalf of manifest or secret sin—will not only attend church services regularly, but will remain at attention in their places until the end of the Divine Liturgy. The zeal that the congregation will show for conscious participation in church services will increase greatly when the priest encourages the faithful to chant out loud for at least some parts of the Divine Liturgy and other holy services, in order to aid in the systematic development and explanation of the rites taking place in the church. When the voices of hundreds of Christians are united into one melody under the direction of the chanter and rise up to God as acceptable incense, and the atmosphere of the church vibrates from the hymns being sung superbly by the entire congregation—young and old, men and women, rich and poor—then not only will it prove impossible for someone to lose his focus and become sidetracked with other thoughts foreign to the holy service being celebrated, but everyone will have an even greater sense that they truly comprise "the body of Christ and each one of them is a part of it." It is incomprehensible and in fact terrible for us to be deprived of the great advantage of having the entire congregation participate in the hymns being sung in church while the heterodox remain more faithful than us in upholding the practices of the ancient Church, which is characterized by its zeal and which we envy. They currently enjoy this privilege, which helps make their holy services so much more vivid. We have envied them on countless occasions when we have found ourselves standing in their colossal churches, which are filled to capacity with faithful parishioners, and our hair stood on end from the sentiments we felt at the sight of all the faithful, from the youngest to the oldest, singing all together. It is true, as one may argue, that it proves difficult for the voices of all the parishioners to come together in sync and form one symphony. However, this argument is automatically refuted when one considers that by expanding catechetical schools all throughout Greece, the Christian faithful will from a very early age become familiarized with the practice of singing at least the most common hymns of the Church, as mentioned above. Everything depends on the zeal that priests everywhere will show on behalf of the salvation of the souls of the faithful.

By all the means mentioned above, and especially by his rich teachings, exhortations, encouragement, and constant instruction, a priest ought to heal the other very grave evil mentioned above: the faithful departing from the holy church prior to the end of the Divine Liturgy. Canon 9 of the Holy Apostles clearly states, "All those faithful who enter and listen to the Scriptures, but who do not stay for prayer and Holy Communion, must be excommunicated, on the ground that they are causing the Church a breach of order." Consider how much we have departed from this express instruction coming from an apostolic canon!

We cannot help but once again call to mind everything that takes place among the heterodox regarding this point as well. Among them it is inconceivable for a Christian to leave prior to the end of the Divine Liturgy, and especially before the clergy exit the holy sanctuary and the area in front of the holy altar, where the Liturgy takes place. Only when the priest goes up to the sacristy with the holy chalice, *diskos*, and veils in hand do the Christians get up from their seats in complete silence and with enviable order in order to exit the holy church. In our parts, others come in "to light a candle" and then leave, others leave after the Gospel reading, others following the Great Entrance, and others on different occasions do so whenever they please! This is clear and convincing proof that our Christian faithful are devoid of every understanding surrounding the Most Holy Sacrament of the Divine Eucharist, which represents the heart of the Divine Liturgy, and that the outward forms that they adhere to do not possess any meaning. Who is at fault for this? We clergymen, the spiritual leaders of our Christian flock. Proof of this lies again in the fact that everywhere that the necessary effort was made on behalf of the clergy, this great evil was corrected.

Furthermore, a priest is obliged to follow the ancient order of the Church and distribute Holy Communion to all those who are going to receive at the moment that he appears before the Beautiful Gate and invites the faithful to approach by saying, "With the fear of God, faith, and love, draw near." The unforgivable mistake of giving Communion to the faithful after the Divine Liturgy, precisely at the moment when the priest or bishop is distributing the *antidoron* amidst disorder, noise, and chatter in the church, makes a mockery of the Most Precious Body and Blood of our Lord Jesus Christ. Who is at fault for this as well? We are, solely and exclusively. Undoubtedly, we will have to answer for this before the awesome judgment seat of God, because by allowing this most disrespectful offense to continue—which incidentally leaves members of other faiths, as well as our fellow Orthodox brethren from the Slavic nations, aghast—we triumphantly and officially set the example of faithlessness and impiety of the most shocking nature. The ancient Church of the seven ecumenical councils that took place during the first eight centuries of its history, to which we always refer members of other denominations, justifiably expecting that they conform themselves to the faith and traditions outlined therein, did not recognize the practice of giving Communion to the faithful following the end of the Divine Liturgy. As the Canon 9 of the Holy Apostles, which we cited above, clearly states, "All those faithful who enter and listen to the Scriptures, but do not stay for prayer and Holy Communion must be excommunicated, on the ground that they are causing the Church a breach of order." Therefore, all those who attend the Divine Liturgy ought to partake of the Blessed Sacrament. Zonaras adds the following at the end of the interpretation of this canon: "For even the laity then were required to partake continually." Balsamon follows with his interpretation of the canon: "The ordainment of the present Canon is very acrid; for it excommunicates those attending church but not staying to the end nor partaking." Because everyone received Communion, there is no doubt that Holy Communion was given at the arranged time as foreseen in the Divine Liturgy, that is, when the priest stands at the Beautiful Gate with the Holy Chalice in hand and says, "With the fear of God, faith, and love, draw near." Therefore, is it not appropriate that this beautiful order observed in the ancient Church be strictly adhered to without the slightest deviation? In doing so, upon seeing the faithful receive Communion, those who do not receive will become cognizant of the great omission they are committing and feel sorrow and contrition over their inferior position as compared to their privileged brethren, and thus their zeal will be stoked so that they might come and partake of the divine sacraments more frequently.

PART 5

THE PASTORAL WORK OF A PRIEST

CHAPTER 1

Its Importance and Meaning

The two previously examined perspectives of a priest's service—the educational and sacerdotal parts—must be topped off with the pastoral perspective. Without the latter, the first two remain incomplete and are critically lacking. A priest has before him a three-front battle against sin and on behalf of the salvation of his flock. If the central battalion—the sacerdotal work—represents the most significant force in the battle, inasmuch as it proceeds head-on in the achievement of its mission, the works of the two other wings—the educational and pastoral work—are of no less use and benefit. Victory and its rewards belong to the minister of the Church who will throw himself into the good fight, ready to take on the enemy and reach the finish line—the salvation of the souls of his flock—while heading with the same speed and attention in all three of the aforementioned directions. Therefore, a priest's pastoral work is significant. Through it his threefold ministry becomes complete and is perfected in form.

The very words of the Savior and preeminent Good Shepherd Himself give the meaning and essence of pastoral work. Christ says that the shepherd of the sheep "calls his own sheep by name and leads them out. When he has brought out all his own, he goes on ahead of them . . . I am the good shepherd. The good shepherd lays down His life for the sheep . . . I am the good shepherd; I know my sheep and My sheep know me . . . and I lay down my life for the sheep. The reason my Father loves Me is that I lay down my life" (John 10:3–4, 11, 14–15, 17). Therefore, acquainting oneself with each and every Christian for the purpose of attending to their spiritual and even material needs, and the general display of welfare on their behalf as spiritual children, should reach as far as self-denial and self-sacrifice. Behold, this is essence and meaning of pastoral work according to the words of the Lord.

Therefore, it is not enough for a priest to teach the faithful, offer them the catechism, and sanctify them. Nor must he consider his work to be complete and his ministry to be fulfilled by performing the above. He must know those entrusted to him by name, as well as their complete moral state. He must also care for them, as a father does for his children, modeling himself upon the Good Shepherd.

CHAPTER 2

Welfare for the Individual

(a) ***Our Lord's Example*** – By reading about the earthly ministry of our Savior Jesus Christ in the books of the Gospel, there is ample proof of the exceptional care that He displayed for each of His disciples and followers. Our Lord teaches the multitudes, feeds thousands of people, speaks to the twelve apostles, and in general works miracles and performs His ministry by making the crowds of people the object of His energies. Nevertheless, at the same time, he displays exceeding care for them as individuals as well. He beckons His disciples and apostles individually, calling them one at a time. He teaches and trains each one with love and patience to do the work of the gospel, correcting them, encouraging them, consoling them, reproving them, and making them wiser. He engages in a long discussion with a Jewish leader named Nicodemus and attempts to convince him of the need for man to be reborn from water and the Spirit. He does not disinterestedly walk by the Samaritan woman, but speaks to her in a familiar tone and draws her in, telling her details about her earlier life with divine accuracy in order to make her a godly herald and apostle of His splendid teaching—the very source of "water welling up to eternal life." He sympathizes with the woman who was caught committing adultery and feels pity for her, magnanimously forgiving her and instructing her to "go, and sin no more." He blesses the sinful woman who anointed His feet with myrrh and washed them with her hair, promising her salvation, and did likewise for Zacchaeus the rich tax collector, who promised to restore those whom he had done injustice to fourfold. What else do the Parables of the Prodigal Son, the Lost Sheep, the Lost Coin testify to if not the special care of which the Savior thought even the worst sinner worthy? He treats the treacherous disciple with paternal care until the very end, and even at the last moment He tries to save him from the abyss of perdition to which he is unstoppably headed.

When in His all-knowing wisdom He realizes that His rebuking will lead to the salvation of those whom He loves, He does not refrain from using harsh and unrelenting language. He tells Peter, "Get behind Me, Satan! You are an offense to Me, for you are not mindful of the things of God, but the things of men" (Matt. 16:23), in an attempt to dissuade him from dying along with Him on the cross, as His Divinity had foreseen. When the Disciples James and John were incensed by the inhospitableness of the Samaritan village that rejected the Savior, they asked Him, "'Lord, do You want us to command fire to come down from heaven and consume them, just as Elijah did?' But He turned and rebuked them, and said, 'You do not know what manner of spirit you are of'" (Luke 9:54–55).

There are many more passages in the Gospel books that demonstrate the love that the Lord felt and openly expressed to isolated individuals. Regarding the rich young man, it is said that "Jesus, looking at him, loved him" (Mark 10:21). Regarding Lazarus' family, it is written that "Now Jesus loved Martha and her sister and Lazarus" (John 11:5). These examples reveal that the strong love that the Lord felt for all the people together and each person in particular was sometimes demonstrated in a more intense manner due to the circumstances that arose, without this meaning that He favored some people over others. Finally, it should be mentioned that during His agony and the frightful pain He experienced upon the cross, He turned His attention to His Most Holy Mother and turned her over to the loving care of His beloved disciple.

(b) ***St. Paul the Apostle's Example*** – Moving on to St. Paul, the Apostle of the Nations, who is full of self-sacrifice, we see that he displays similar pastoral care for each and every one of those who believed in the gospel. Addressing the church elders in Ephesus, he says to them, among other things, "For three years I did not cease to warn everyone night and day with tears" (Acts 20:31) and "I kept back nothing that was helpful, but proclaimed it to you, and taught you publicly and from house to house" (Acts 20:20). From these words, the welfare that he displayed for not only the entire flock, but for each family and individual, is evident. It is precisely this rigidly exact and zealous performance of apostolic duty that made him able to declare, although imprisoned, that "I have fought the good fight, I have finished the race, I have kept the faith. Finally, there is laid up for me the crown of righteousness" (2 Tim. 4:7–8). Likewise, in a Letter to the Thessalonians, he writes the following with special emphasis: "You are witnesses, and God also, how devoutly and justly and blamelessly we behaved ourselves among you who believe; as you know how we exhorted, and comforted, and charged every one of you, as a father does his own children, that you would walk worthy of God who calls you into His own kingdom and glory" (1 Thess. 2:10–12). How great indeed is the pastoral care that is displayed on behalf of the individual in this famous passage from his Letter to the Thessalonians! In order not to get too caught up in the efforts and struggles that St. Paul put forth for the pastoral instruction of his disciples Titus and Timothy, and the care that he displayed on behalf of Onesimus the slave, considering it not unworthy of his time to write an entire letter about him to Philemon, we cite his words to the Christian faithful in Colossae regarding preaching about Christ: "Him we preach, warning every man and teaching every man in all wisdom, that we may present every man perfect in Christ Jesus. To this end I also labor, striving according to His working which works in me mightily" (Col. 1:28–29). Here we have the model of a true shepherd, who does not limit himself to caring for the flock in its entirety, but considers himself responsible for warning each person and teaching each person, that he may present every person perfect in Christ Jesus.

With the example of the Good Shepherd and St. Paul the Apostle in mind, in addition to the pastoral work of the multitude of holy fathers of the Church, who showed themselves to be faithful copies of the divine archetype through their zeal and self-denial, a priest is obliged to diligently fulfill his pastoral work, which, as detailed above, consists of displaying welfare to the individual. "He who is entrusted with caring for the common good must be so inclined as if obliged to give an account for each of the persons entrusted to him," St. Basil the Great says.

CHAPTER 3

Conditions for the Fulfillment of Pastoral Work

Pastoral work worthy of a priest who has received his calling from Christ is impossible to comprehend devoid of ***divine zeal***, which stokes the fire of the soul and leads to action and work. The entire existence of a pastor in Christ must be burning with the fire of this zeal on behalf of the glory of God and the salvation of mankind. "I came to send fire on the earth, and how I wish it were already kindled!" (Luke 12:49) said our Lord, alluding to the divine fire for the spreading of the Christian proclamation, which He instilled in the hearts of His disciples and apostles, and through them to the priests of His Church. Jeremiah the Prophet testifies to the fact that He wanted His instruments like this, when he says, "'Behold, I will send for many fishermen,' says the Lord, 'and they shall fish them; and afterward I will send for many hunters, and they shall hunt them'" (Jer. 16:16). The pastoral work of a priest that is lacking in zeal is lifeless, insipid, and feeble. Zeal begets enthusiasm, without which there can be nothing that is great and lasting, according to Emerson. A spiritual pastor who is inspired by zeal and enthusiasm can work miracles for his flock and change the face of his parish. He passes on his strength to the souls of his spiritual children and becomes all things to all men, for the sake of one thought only and one ideal: to glorify God by saving the Christians entrusted to his spiritual care. In his wonderful oration on St.

Athanasius the Great, St. Gregory the Theologian describes the godly zeal of this great man—a true giant of the Church—and illustrates his tireless care for all: "Let the virgins celebrate the friend of the Bridegroom; those under the yoke their restrainer, hermits him who lent wings to their course, cenobites their lawgiver, simple folk their guide, contemplatives the divine, the joyous their bridle, the unfortunate their consolation, the hoary-headed their staff, youths their instructor, the poor their resource, the wealthy their steward. Even the widows will, methinks, praise their protector, even the orphans their father, even the poor their benefactor, strangers their entertainer, brethren the man of brotherly love, the sick their physician, in whatever sickness or treatment you will, the healthy the guard of health, yea all men him who made himself all things to all men that he might gain almost, if not quite, all" (NPNF[2] 7:272; PG 35:1093). "I have become all things to all men, that I might by all means save some" (1 Cor. 9:22), St. Paul exclaims. It was this sort of sacred and fervent zeal that St. John Chrysostom had in mind when he said that one man is enough to change an entire city. How true indeed! Wherever there has been a major religious awakening that has taken place and wherever the people have cast away the slumber of indifference and the lethargy of aloofness, returning to Christ with their hearts and souls and attaining new heights of Christian works; wherever a spiritual movement of this sort has taken place and has lived on for entire centuries, affecting generations and generations of people, the main leaders were clergymen filled with zeal and fervor. The zealot pastor remains ever vigilant so he may watch over his flock. Even when he rests after the day's work is done, his thoughts remain on his mission. He goes over all that has taken place and notes what was lacking, so he may undertake his service the next day with greater strength and even more zeal.

A foreign contemporary, inspired, religious poet writes:

The day is reaching its end.
What good works have I presented before You, Lord,
since its beginning, as an offering for my holy ministry?
What evils did I defeat, what good did I uphold?
What fight have I fought, and which victory have I won?
What good did I attempt to do, and what did I achieve?

I am weak, even when I put forth strenuous efforts!
I see, but I cannot reach the luminous peak that always lies ahead of me.
And although I always and continuously think that I have reached it,
I feel my weak hands go limp,
and devoid of all courage, I fall back into the darkness!
Because You have given me both of these, effort and disheartenment,
for the sake of Your mission
(Longfellow)

Humility must go hand in hand with zeal. Without it, our work will not be blessed by God, and our efforts will not bear fruit and will be scattered. Regardless of the number of successes that we may attain, and as many achievements as may crown our pastoral efforts, we ought to avoid boasting and bragging about them. The heavenly St. Paul, who "was caught up to the third heaven and heard inexpressible words, which it is not lawful for a man to utter" (2 Cor. 12:2, 4), he who became a chosen vessel and received the gospel that he preached "neither ... from man ... but ... through the revelation of Jesus Christ" (Gal. 1:12), in spite of all this calls himself "one untimely born" (1 Cor. 15:8), "the least of the apostles" (1 Cor. 15:9), "less than the least of all the saints" (Eph. 3:8) and attributes all his apostolic success to the grace of God (1 Cor. 15:10) and further testifies that even his efforts and labors are the result of the grace of God in him: "I labored more abundantly than they all, yet not I, but the grace of God which was with me" (1 Cor. 15:10). St. Peter, amazed at the great number of fish he had caught, which was due to the intervention of the divine Fisher of souls, cried out, "Depart from me, for I am a sinful man, O Lord!" (Luke 5:8). St. John Chrysostom, who illuminated the entire universe with his life and timeless writings, considered himself unworthy of priesthood and full of shortcomings. "For my soul is weak and puny," he writes in his work *On the Priesthood* (NPNF[1] 9:80; PG 48:646). So, after all this, today's minister of the Church must ask himself how he should think of himself and his possible successes in the office of priesthood.

Every success and every perfect gift comes from God and is due to Him. Therefore, let us wait to receive praise from God. "He who boasts is to boast in the Lord. For it is not he who commends himself that is approved, but he whom the Lord commends" (2 Cor. 10:17–18). Let a priest never wish to boast about his sermon, the order he keeps in the church, and his charitable works, nor put down the work done by his predecessors, even if their contribution was but small and worth only a few words. Besides, what often occurs is that of which St. Paul speaks, alluding to braggarts who are so amazed by the miniscule things that they accomplish, but which make them think that there is no one who can compare to them. "But they, measuring themselves by themselves, and comparing themselves among themselves, are not wise" (2 Cor. 10:12).

St. Gregory the Theologian writes, "If, I say, we have furnished ourselves with two or three expressions of pious authors, and that by hearsay, not by study; if we have had a brief experience of David . . . we are at once wise teachers, of high estimation in Divine things, the first of scribes and lawyers; we ordain ourselves men of heaven and seek to be called Rabbi by men; . . . and we should be annoyed if we were not lauded to excess" (NPNF[2] 7:215; PG 35:457). Elsewhere he adds, "And we may rightly, in my opinion, apply to them the saying of Solomon: There is an evil which I have seen under the sun [Eccl 10:5], a man wise in his own conceit [Prov 26:12]; and a still greater evil is to charge with the instruction of others a man who is not even aware of his own ignorance" (NPNF[2] 7:215; PG 35:460). Further down he states, "Vain glory is a great hindrance to men's attainment of virtue" (NPNF[2] 7:215; PG 35:461). Despite the prolific ministry that he has to show for himself, a good pastor will always recall the words of St. Paul, which were uttered on another occasion but are nonetheless fitting: "But one thing I do, forgetting those things which are behind and reaching forward to those things which are ahead, I press toward the goal for the prize of the upward call of God in Christ Jesus" (Phil. 3:13–14). He will also not attend to his spiritual flock as if a salaried employee at some job or in a vainglorious manner, but with humility and in fear and awe, working on behalf of their salvation.

Zeal and humility must be accompanied by pastoral ***prudence***, which sets the pastor's zeal in the right direction. Zeal that is lacking in prudence becomes a bearer of evils, and often it is capable of destroying years of work over just a short period of time. Zeal without prudence leads to extreme situations, creates dangerous fanaticism, blinds the person whom it possesses, and leads him to lose face and dignity. The Bible says that the Lord appeared to Solomon in a dream and said to him, "Ask! What shall I give you?" And Solomon, who was unmatched in wisdom by anyone coming before him or after him, answered, "I am a little child; I do not know how to go out or come in. And Your servant is in the midst of Your people whom You have chosen, a great people, too numerous to be numbered or counted. Therefore, give to Your servant an understanding heart to judge Your people, that I may discern between good and evil" (1 Kgs. 3:7–9). Behold, here is the prayer that a pastor ought to repeat over and over again. By the word "prudence," we do not mean to suggest backing down over anything for the sake of securing the love and favor of the people. No! There are instances when the greatness of God and the salvation of the people demand that we persist in our course until the very end. In these sorts of situations, pastoral prudence itself demands persistence, stability, and boldness.

The great examples of St. John Chrysostom, who mercilessly lashed out at Eudoxia and the licentious minions of lay people and clergymen surrounding her at court; or St. Ambrose, who refused to offer Holy Communion to the mighty Byzantine emperor Theodosius, whose hands were dripping with the blood of Christians from Thessaloniki; or St. Basil the Great, who rebuked the prefect Modestus with courage and boldness; and any other similar ancient or modern-day examples from the history of the Church are most educational lessons, demonstrating where and when a good pastor can combine prudence with zeal.

Finally, ***love***—the pinnacle of all virtues—must stand out as the chief characteristic and virtue of a good pastor. A pastor must not discriminate among his flock. Rather, all—rich and poor, civic leaders and private individuals, officials and everyday folks—must be the object of his pastoral care. Especially those who are lost in the crowd, the poor, those who are worn down, the common folk, those who look to their spiritual father as their only supporter and defender—they must enjoy special attention. Love must guide the priest to seek out those who have fallen astray, who have estranged themselves from the Church, who are walking in the valley of the shadow of death, and bear upon them the open wounds of sin. "What do you think? If a man has a hundred sheep, and one of them goes astray, does he not leave the ninety-nine and go to the mountains to seek the one that is straying?" (Matt. 18:12). Love, which is manifested through graciousness of manners and approachability, ought to govern a pastor's relations with his flock, but of course under no circumstances is it to be perceived as flattery and an attempt to curry favor with others. "One should be affable in conversation and agreeable in social intercourse, not resorting to wit as a means of gaining popularity, but depending upon the charm which comes from gracious politeness. On all occasions abjure asperity, even when it is necessary to administer a rebuke" (St. Basil the Great, *Letter 2*, in *Saint Basil: The Letters*, 18).

CHAPTER 4

Pastoral Work

Confession

And now we reach the very essence of pastoral service. We defined it above as being the special welfare that a priest shows for each and every Christian. A priest must attend to the flock under his care as individuals, inside the church during Holy Confession, as well as outside of it by visiting those who are laid up in bed, caring for those in need, and regularly monitoring all who have been entrusted to him.

The confessional is a priest's spiritual workplace, in which he succeeds in bringing about the spiritual salvation of his flock. During his teaching, the priest plants the seeds of the moral truths of Christianity, and when he hears confessions, he reaps and harvests the fruits of his educational labors. He casts the net from the pulpit, but the fish are caught in the confessional. It is there that the pastor will see the souls that are destined to remain animated all throughout his priestly career be uplifted, but at the same time his pastoral heart will feel pain, inexpressible sorrow, and even revulsion in the face of sin, which he will encounter in all its repugnance and ugliness. For the most part, the latter feelings will trouble his soul, because the confessional is the hospital in which those who are morally ill come to have their illness and wounds examined, and receive treatment. The pastor is a healer of souls. It is there that the priest will see the horror of hell and the radiance and allure of heaven. He will march into the dark soul of the sinner and take pleasure in the innocence of the soul of a child. He will witness the compunction and genuine repentance of the prodigal son who has returned home, and he will come face to face with the self-complacent egotism of those who worship outwardly and out of habit—those who are not cognizant of their own condition. He will rejoice upon hearing the unfeigned confession of the forthright and the poor in spirit, and he will feel depression at the sight of the immodesty displayed by those possessed by a spirit of secularism and unbridled materialism. But, as we said earlier, the priest is a spiritual doctor who heals souls, and being endowed with the virtues listed above, he ought to display patience and forbearance, and become, in the words of St. Paul, to the weak as weak, that he might win the weak. He has become all things to all men, that he might by all means save some (1 Cor. 9:22). Hearing the confessions of his spiritual children with all forbearance, he is obliged to tell them everything that they must hear, advise them, console them, and also reprove and rebuke them. However, in doing so, he must feel sorrow for the sinner and empathize with his condition, precisely as a biological father suffers along with and empathizes with his beloved child when he is suffering or in pain. "In regards to those who heal the souls . . . the speaker himself suffers first, whenever he would admonish others" St. John Chrysostom says.

To bring up a specific example, here is how a spiritual father might go about his work when faced with the instance of a Christian who has sinned.

He should recall the beautiful times when the person making his confession was a child, when he would enter the Church with a clean conscience to worship God with a pure soul and sing hymns of praise and supplication to the Most High with innocent lips.

Then, as a skillful spiritual surgeon, he will place the sharp scalpel of admonition into the root of the most severe of the sins that the repentant person has confessed, while leaving aside the smaller and less significant ones, not because the latter do not affect the spiritual health and well-being of the Christian, but primarily because the repentant person must not be brought to a state of hopelessness upon hearing such a large number of offenses stacked up against him from the lips of his spiritual father. Secondly, and most importantly—simply put—by striking down the chief sin, its offshoots will also be struck simultaneously, and when the leader is eliminated, the secondary accomplices and the instruments of the sinful gang eating away at the poor soul that stumbled upon them will be scattered and doomed to idleness.

He will then describe the tragic consequences of sin upon the body, and above all upon the soul, and he will remind the person making the confession of the frightful moment of death and judgment, when all things will have to appear open and laid bare before the judgment seat of the impartial Judge. Therefore, would he want to appear before the Lord in such a state? What if he were called shortly, at this very moment, to appear before Him?

He will then compare the infinite mercy of God with the unworthiness and baseness of man, and he will encourage the sinner and fill him with hope and solace, telling him that the Lord is ready and always willing at every moment to receive us in repentance, provided that we try not to return to our previous life of sin. It might also be mentioned that the moment of confession stands as a singular opportunity given by God for the salvation of the repentant soul. He loves, forgives, forbears, forgets, and eagerly awaits the blessed hour when the sinner will decide to return (see the Parable of the Prodigal Son, the Lost Sheep, the Lost Coin, etc.).

CHAPTER 5

The Sick

Part of pastoral service—no less important and requiring zeal, sympathy, and love on the part of the pastor—involves visiting the sick. The fact that we have overlooked this duty on our part and in time removed it from the list of a priest's responsibilities altogether may contribute to the feeling of surprise we get when hearing about pastoral obligations involving the sick. In spite of all this, in countries inhabited by Christians belonging to other denominations, this is considered one of a parish priest's most essential duties, and it is impossible to conceive of a minister of the Most High who does not dedicate some time from his day to fulfilling the obligation of visiting his sick parishioners to console, encourage, and prepare them for the eternal life that exists beyond the grave. Indeed, how true this is. The public life of Christ while on earth stands as our eternal model, and so we have a duty as His servants to emulate it in all things. The majority of Christ's time was spent in the service of those who suffered. He gave sight to the blind, raised the paralytics, cleansed lepers, and resurrected the dead. Summing up Christ's public ministry, St. Matthew the Evangelist writes, "Then Jesus went about all the cities and villages . . . healing every sickness and every disease among the people" (9:35). "Whatever city you enter . . . heal the sick there" (Luke 10:8–9), the Lord said to His disciples and apostles. He pronounces those who visited the sick worthy of the kingdom of heaven (Matt. 25:36).

Visiting the sick gives the priest a singular opportunity to exercise spiritual influence and win them over to Christ if they are strangers to Him and indifferent to His teachings, or strengthen them if they are faithful children of the Church, so that they may courageously face the painful moments of their illness and succumb to physical death—which is a liberation and transport from sorrowful things to more pleasant ones—in faith and unshakable Christian hope. There is more. Visits by the priest to the sick—especially during critical moments in their illness and in instances of incurable diseases that are contagious—raises his stature in the eyes of those who are observing all his interaction with the sick Christians and strengthens the prestige and social mission of the Church in their minds. Finally, it fills them with courage and places in their souls the sweet hope that during the difficult moments in their life they can always count on the ready help and support of their spiritual fathers. These sorts of thoughts and feelings are unbreakable bonds that connect the flock with their pastors. "When people see the priest walking in heavy rain to a humble home where a sick Christian is laid up; when they see him leave his dinner table and bed and walk across rough roads and dark pathways in the middle of the night to be with a sick person; when they see that a contagious disease does not scare him, but rather that he calmly and fearlessly stays by the bedside of those who are burning with fever and writhing from the pain of a dangerous disease; when they see him kneeling alongside their beloved child, father, or mother and displaying through his entire manner the care and mercy that Jesus Christ showed those who suffered; when they see him repeatedly visit the home of a sick person so that he may offer greater solace and secure the salvation of the sick person—then they will feel joy and pride, because they belong to the Church which that particular priest represents. The sick will eagerly await his visit and will believe firmly in him because of all of the above, because they will see that he too believes all that he teaches and preaches beyond the shadow of a doubt," says a bishop of a foreign Church.

It is a fact that in our land there is an unacceptable belief, which is foreign to the Christian spirit, against the presence of a priest in the home of a sick person. Although it is frightful to say(!), in these types of circumstances the priest is considered to be a harbinger and precursor to death. We must admit that even the sick person himself, who has grown up and lived in an environment where similar ideas prevail, is overcome with fear as soon as he sees a minister of the Church standing over his bed, and this fear grows greater and reaches its peak if some of the more devout members of the family suggest that the ill person receive the holy sacraments due to the acute nature of the malady. However, this fear and foolish superstition should be uprooted from the souls of the Christian faithful; and this depends entirely upon the clergy. Truth be told, I envy the Christian faithful and clergy in England, where a priest considers it his duty to pay regular visits to the hospitals and homes where sick members of his flock are receiving treatment. They too, during their time of illness, eagerly await for the priest's visit, so they may speak familiarly and as friends with him, and take the opportunity to ask him any questions they may have on various religious and ethical matters. It should also be noted that in the Anglican Church paying regular visits to the sick is a pressing and mandatory duty of every priest that cannot be ignored, much less avoided. Rather than wasting valuable time to no avail, the parish priest will always make visits to his parishioners during the afternoon with the aim of holding an edificational conversation with them, and he will always prefer to visit those of his parishioners who are sick.

I believe that it is possible for this practice to be done here as well, and for it to be made known to the faithful through sermons in church, written notifications, and visits to homes that the priest's presence at the bedside of a sick person is imperative and is called for by the very spirit and essence of our religion, together with love and care for the sick person, as well as his family and friends. It could be appropriately emphasized to the faithful that an illness should be seen as a warning by the All-Merciful God that our stay on this earth is only temporary, and that it is our duty and in our best interests to be spiritually ready to face death. If the things of the present that are visible to us now are nothing in comparison to what the "eye has not seen, nor ear heard, nor have entered into the heart of man the things which God has prepared for those who love Him" (1 Cor. 2:9), is this not justification enough to make every attempt to refute this misguided belief, and does not every effort—even the most painstaking one—seem small and insignificant so that this anti-Christian superstition may be wiped out and this unfounded fear be cast away? The death of an unrepentant sinner is a bottomless pit of spiritual doom, and the edge of this cliff is the bed upon which he is sprawled. The salvation, thanks to which the ill sinner will enjoy eternal delight and ineffable bliss, depends firstly, of course, on his free will and his desire to repent and return back from the inhospitable land of sin to the home of his father, from where he originally left. However, this also depends on those who surround him—parents, siblings, a spouse. These people are capable of offering the greatest gift and the most valuable service to their loved one by calling the devout and zealous parish priest to his bedside and working together with this minister of the Church so that their sick friend or relative may be saved during the last days of his earthly life and may leave this world happy, so that he may enter the life of eternal bliss.

It goes without saying that no small amount of skill and pastoral experience is needed so that a visit to a sick person ends up being effective. During the humble performance of my duties as the parish priest of the Greek immigrants in London, I was given many opportunities to visit Greeks who were sick. I can say that not a week would go by without me making one or two visits to Greeks who were ill. From all that I had read and seen by observing the social work of the Anglicans, I learned a lot, and I attempted to implement what I had learned from reading and my own personal experiences. So, during my first visit, the discussion would revolve around the patient's occupation, lifestyle, and family situation. During my second visit, I would ask the patient if he attended church, if he read Scripture, how many times a year he received communion, and if he would like to receive Holy Communion now during his time of illness. On many occasions, my feeble efforts were crowned with success by divine grace and condescension, and I saw no small number of sick Christians who loved the gospel of Jesus Christ and were interested in it. I always attempted to offer them copies of the Holy Bible and other edificational books. Among the people I visited, there were also some who, although suffering from serious illnesses and facing a bleak future, I did not manage to convince to receive Communion. During these instances, my efforts stumbled against the deeply rooted belief that Holy Communion foreshadows death. If these poor souls knew that physical death is unavoidable, but that it is possible to temper its pain and avoid the terrible danger of the eternal death of the soul, they certainly would not have made the flimsy and foolish arguments that they used to reject the Bread of life being offered to them. May the Lord grant rest to their souls in His infinite mercy.

So, a priest must visit his sick parishioners and try—in instances of chronic illness—to instill in them the idea that he is a true friend to them who is greatly interested in both their physical and spiritual health. During the period of the patient's illness, a priest must view his objective goal to be the patient's rebirth in Christ—if the situation involves a Christian who has not been born again through confession and partaking of the Holy Sacraments. Every conversation with the patient must lead toward this end. In other words, together with the doctor overseeing the patient's body, the priest—as a spiritual doctor—must look over his spiritual child, who is being challenged by this illness, and must help in the healing effort by offering the appropriate spiritual medicine, which benefits a patient by bringing about salvation.

CHAPTER 6

The Poor

Every benevolent undertaking and every philanthropic action in the parish must always revolve around the parish priest, who is the axis of these efforts. He represents Him who repeatedly called the poor blessed (Matt. 5:3; Luke 6:20); who promised His heavenly kingdom to those who cared for people in need (Matt. 25:35); and who, although rich, became poor for our sake, so that we might become rich through His poverty (2 Cor. 8:9). St. John Chrysostom says that poverty "becomes God's mask. God is hidden in poverty. Although [it appears to be] a beggar, with hands outstretched, it is God who is accepting" the alms.

It is impossible to imagine a spiritual father who is not charitable. The priest stands as a symbol of self-denial and self-sacrifice in the parish. Everyone looks to him as the spiritual figure whom they will turn to during their time of need to address their material needs as well. However many and whatever sort of personal and family needs that a priest has, he has a duty to always be the first to set a good example by offering relief to the poor, together with support and aid to the less fortunate. Therefore, let the love of money—the root of all evils (1 Tim. 6:10)—be foreign to him, for it is detested even among the laity, and becomes a cause of shame for the Church and spiritual destruction when the spiritual father bears this characteristic. A greedy priest becomes an obstacle that trips up his flock, and the root of the scandal affecting them. Judas was destroyed by avarice. This shortcoming makes men who were destined to become pillars of the Church and bastions of the congregation in light of their position and intellectual ability worthless and destroys them. How can a greedy man of the cloth fight against this despicable vice if he cannot repeat the words of St. Paul: "Silver and gold I do not have" (Acts 3:6)? Moreover, what sort of belief can a priest have in divine providence if he accumulates money and various other material goods for fear of poverty and deprivation? Of course, he is allowed and obliged to attend to relatives of his who may be needy, but it is in itself criminal for him to overlook the poor people in his parish or local area who have been entrusted to him by God, for the sole purpose of making his relatives prosperous. In such a case, the clergyman becomes like all the rest who do not have hope, and he has entered the clergy not because of any special calling and enthusiasm for saving souls and glorifying God, but for the purpose of serving ignoble intentions, thus scandalizing the consciences of the faithful and dooming himself to eternal damnation. The priest should always keep in mind the famous precepts that St. Paul passed down to Timothy in his letter: "For we brought nothing into this world, and it is certain we can carry nothing out. And having food and clothing, with these we shall be content. But those who desire to be rich fall into temptation and a snare, and into many foolish and harmful lusts which drown men in destruction and perdition" (1 Tim. 6:7–9).

By giving whatever, he can of his own possessions, a priest will exercise his pastoral influence upon rich parishioners and invite them to offer some relief to their poor brethren. Love for the poor should be a favorite topic for church sermons, and the priest should make frequent reference to it, thus manifesting his love and active interest for them.

A spiritual father who is active and zealous is capable of making the Church a center and hub of effective philanthropy. He can also call upon devout and charitable men and women to assist him, and with their help organize the parish's philanthropic efforts systematically, so that every poor person may find assistance readily, and no person who is truly worthy of support may leave the Church empty-handed. This sort of organized philanthropy, with an entire network of methodical efforts that spread all across the parish, will help avoid mistakes that can cause harm to the very people for whom the aid is intended. In certain instances, the parish may offer food, clothing, heating supplies, and so forth in lieu of money, which always carries with it the suspicion that the receiver may choose to spend it aimlessly, opting to gratify needs of a secondary nature and importance. A priest should elect to aid virtuous people leading a Christian life over people who have proven themselves to be bad and irreverent. It is not uncommon for the poverty of the latter to have resulted from a life of impropriety, filled with excesses and abuses that go directly against the true spirit of Christianity. The priest should watch over the poor and try to find work for all those whose poverty is the result of unemployment, thus allowing them to earn a living for themselves. The priest will serve as the heart and soul of this movement. He is the one who will know all the poor by name and take measures to ensure that poverty does not lead them to commit sins or undermine their morals, nor lead them to become hopeless and lose their souls.

CHAPTER 7

The Healthy

In defining the meaning of pastoral service, we wrote above that it consists of the priest acquainting himself with each individual Christian, with the ultimate goal being the salvation of their souls. "I know my sheep and am known of mine." But how will the pastor come to know those who have been entrusted to him? It so happens that many of them do not attend church or go to Holy Confession. The sick and the poor, whom we spoke of earlier, are special and exceptional cases in a priest's pastoral service. On the other hand, even if we are to assume that all the Christian faithful more or less come to the parish to worship, and come to confession at certain periods during the year, a pastor will still not be able to get to know his spiritual children in such a way as to speak familiarly with them, establish friendly relations with them, and generally get to know them in their daily lives, with their virtues and possible shortcomings. A parish priest accomplishes this by visiting the homes of the faithful regularly and during certain periods. It is the duty of a good pastor to not wait for the sheep to instinctively return to him, but to go out in search of them. This is the meaning that the Savior's Parables of the Lost Sheep and the Lost Coin hold. The act of delivering an effective sermon and engaging in the sacrament of confession have as conditions and demand that we develop a deep knowledge of our Christian flock's daily lives. How can it be possible for a priest to teach effectively if he is ignorant of the life, habits, level of intelligence, thoughts, and beliefs of his Christian flock? Besides, during the moment of confession it proves impossible for the priest to get to know his flock from this standpoint. This is achieved only by visiting them at their homes.

A priest who visits his parishioners enhances the material that he will draw upon during his sermons. He knows what direction to steer them in and what points he will stress to give his sermon the spiritual value that will be able to somewhat make up for the lack of erudition and rhetorical skill.

But in visiting our parishioners, we should seek out something greater and more significant as well. We must approach those who are distant from the Church and, through friendly conversation and paternal persuasion, try to win them over and make them faithful children of the Orthodox Church. These people maintain a position of indifference, which is sometimes even cold and hostile to religion, on account of unjustified biases and misguided ideas derived from the influence of people with warped minds and hardened consciences, or from reading books that for undisclosed reasons muddle the truth and present falsehoods instead. These people are good-willed by nature, but are in the darkness of ignorance and under the influence of hostile feelings toward the Church because they never had the opportunity to approach or subjectively avoided interacting with people who were able to influence them beneficially. Here is a singular opportunity for a priest to exercise his pastoral work and save the members of his flock who are led astray in this manner from losing their souls. If in spite of all his efforts he is not able to reach the desired goal, he can at least have a clear conscience and rest assured that he fulfilled his pastoral duty to the best of his ability. "Yet, if you warn the wicked, and he does not turn from his wickedness, nor from his wicked way, he shall die in his iniquity; but you have delivered your soul" (Ezek. 3:19).

Aside from this, though, during his visits a priest should take the opportunity to talk about the religious education of the young children in the home, giving advice on how to raise them in the nurture and admonition of the Lord. He should encourage the parents to send their children to Sunday School and appeal to their moral support for the progress of his catechetical and philanthropic efforts in the parish. In this way, a relationship of love in Christ and sincere friendship will develop between the pastor and his flock, and perhaps changes will come about in the souls of the Christian faithful due to the almighty grace of the Holy Spirit, an explanation of which surpasses our limited mental faculties.

In visiting his parishioners, the priest will serve as a guardian angel upholding the family peace and safeguarding the strict adherence to the unadulterated traditions that have kept the Greek family alive and well for centuries, safe from the influences of foreign pestilence. There are, of course, families in every walk of Greek society who devoutly uphold the values that have been proven to have saved our nation from the countless adversities it has faced over the centuries. In these families, love prevails among spouses, and their mutual relations are governed by genuine affection. Children and parents live together in harmony. Parental authority—which bears no similarity to despotism and imperiousness—is obediently recognized by children, while the children's love is a joy and relief for content parents. Brothers and sisters live together in concert, while bickering, disagreements, and conflicts have no place in the family. Guileless devoutness to God grows and progresses, while not even death can destroy and erase the mutual devotion shared by the members of these blessed families. Christ, the source of all good things and blessings, reigns in the midst of these families.

But there are also other families out there into which the pest of licentiousness and corruption has entered. In families like these, parents and children follow paths that are completely different. The former set a bad example, while the children surpass their parents in moral impropriety. Conflicts, arguments, and squabbles characterize these families. To top off all the evils and the disintegration of the family's core, sons and daughters seeking their freedom leave the family home, or a disastrous divorce—this scourge of modern Greek society—takes place. Here is a field filled with weeds, but opportune for a spiritual father to undertake coordinated work. Here lies an opportunity for a priest to prove himself worthy of his calling, which he followed in order to serve and to live up to the titles of "light of the world" and "salt of the earth." Let no obstacle and no difficulty dispel a pastor's zeal to restore peace and bring back love to these households in tribulation. Let the phrases of St. Paul "Be ready in season and out of season. Convince, rebuke, exhort" and "I did not cease to warn everyone night and day with tears" serve as the standard for the priest's actions in these kinds of circumstances.

But in instances such as these involving souls that have grown distant from God, a great deal of attention is needed on behalf of the pastor in order to return them to the Lord's sheepfold. In exceptional situations such as these, fervent prayer for enlightenment and guidance will help the pastor choose between strict or gentle measures for the correction of those who have been led astray. There is always the grave danger that improper spiritual medicine may bring about more harm than good. As St. John Chrysostom says, "For if you deal too gently with him who needs a severe application of the knife, and do not strike deep into one who requires such treatment, you remove one part of the sore but leave the other: and if on the other hand you make the requisite incision unsparingly, the patient, driven to desperation by his sufferings, will often fling everything away at once, both the remedy and the bandage, and throw himself down headlong, 'breaking the yoke and bursting the band'" (NPNF[1] 9:41). In general, a priest ought to keep in mind the differences in personalities and the different makeup of each Christian, and apply the treatment that suits each one after great consideration, offering the spiritual remedy that benefits each person, just as St. Gregory the Theologian says in his oration on St. Athanasius the Great: "Praising some, gently rebuking others; rousing the sluggishness of these, restraining the passion of those; in some cases, eager to prevent a fall, in others devising means of recovery after a fall; simple in disposition, manifold in the arts of government; clever in argument, cleverer still in mind; condescending to the lowlier, outsoaring the more lofty; hospitable, protector of suppliants" (NPNF[2] 7:280–81; PG 35:1125).

In any case, the spiritual father must follow the example of the Divine Leader, and when he comes across Christians who have been hardened by sin due to their lack of spirituality, he ought to exhaust all his forbearance, gentleness, and his genuine paternal love and care for them, because opposite methods of strict admonition and abrasive disparagement are very likely to bring about results that are completely contrary to what was expected. The person who is wounded by sin and filled with bruises as a result of not leading a life in Christ needs affectionate care, paternal understanding, and behavior that encourages him and does not create desperation and hopelessness over the salvation of his soul. St. John Chrysostom, the great father and a teacher of the Church, is absolutely correct when he observes, "For when once the soul has been forced to put off shame it lapses into a callous condition, and neither yields to kindly words nor bends to threats, nor is susceptible of gratitude, but becomes far worse than that city which the prophet reproached, saying, 'you had the face of a harlot, refusing to be ashamed before all men.' Therefore, the pastor has need of much discretion, and of a myriad eye to observe on every side the habit of the soul" (NPNF[1] 9:41; PG 48:365).

Therefore, a priest must get to the furthest depths of the souls of his Christian flock during confession so that he may relieve them of the weeds of sin that destroy the soul, rendering them pure and suitable for the kingdom of God. He must console the sick and seize the opportunity to see to it that the suffering associated with the illness becomes redemptive for those who are afflicted. He should provide relief to the needy by being the first to set a charitable example and by working together with devout parishioners and benevolent societies. He should be a faithful supporter of families, safeguarding love and peace, which he ought to hold together for the good of the family members. He will do all these things with one mission in mind and one burning desire that guides his thoughts and rouses his energies to action—glorifying God through the salvation of men and women, whom he has set out to teach, sanctify, and shepherd.

THE END

GLORY TO HIM WHO GIVES US LIFE
THROUGH JESUS CHRIST

PUBLICATIONS BY THIS AUTHOR

1. *Life and work in the Diocese of Athens*. London, 1928.

2. *The Orthodox Church*. London, 1931.

3. Ὁ Ἱερεύς. Alexandria. 1931.

4. Βραχὺ σχεδίασμα περὶ τῆς Ἐκκλησίας τῆς Ἀγγλίας. Alexandria, 1931.

5. Ἡ Μίμησις τοῦ Χριστοῦ. Athens, 1933.

6. Ὁ ἐν Λονδίνῳ Ἑλληνικὸς Ὀρθόδοξος Ναός. Oxford, 1933.

7. Βίος καὶ Πολιτεία τοῦ Ὁσίου Πατρὸς ἡμῶν Ἀντωνίου. Alexandria, 1933.

8. Ὁ Μέγας Ἀθανάσιος καὶ ἡ ἐποχὴ αὐτοῦ. Athens, 1937.

9. Ἀγγλικανοὶ καὶ Ὀρθόδοξοι. Athens, 1937.

10. Τὸ Συνέδριον τοῦ Ἐδιμβούργου. Athens, 1938.

11. Συνταγμάτιον κατὰ Παπιστικοῦ Καθαρτηρίου πυρός. Athens, 1939.

12. Ἡ ἐν Χριστῷ Ζωή. 1st ed., New York, 1924; 2nd ed., Athens, 1939.

13. Ἡ Ἱστορία τοῦ Χριστοῦ (γιὰ μικρὰ παιδιά).

14. Θρησκεία καὶ Διανόησις. Corinth, 1946.

15. Ὁ Ἱερεύς. Ἔκδοσις ἐπηυξημένη καὶ βελτιωμένη. Athens, 1946.

CPSIA information can be obtained
at www.ICGtesting.com
Printed in the USA
BVHW091202190723
667422BV00005B/19